Copyright
Plain and
Simple

By
Cheryl Besenjak

CAREER PRESS
3 Tice Road
P.O. Box 687
Franklin Lakes, NJ 07417
1-800-CAREER-1
201-848-0310 (NJ and outside U.S.)
FAX: 201-848-1727

COPYRIGHT PLAIN AND SIMPLE
ISBN 1-56414-273-6, $11.99
Cover design by The Hub Graphics Corp.
Printed in the U.S.A. by Book-mart Press

To order this title by mail, please include price as noted
above, $2.50 handling per order, and $1.50 for each book ordered. Send to: Career Press, Inc., 3 Tice Road, P.O. Box 687,
Franklin Lakes, NJ 07417.

Or call toll-free 1-800-CAREER-1 (NJ and Canada: 201-
848-0310) to order using VISA or MasterCard, or for further
information on books from Career Press.

Library of Congress Cataloging-in-Publication Data
Besenjak, Cheryl, 1949-
    Copyright plain and simple / Cheryl Besenjak.
        p.   cm.
    Includes index.
    ISBN 1-56414-273-6 (pbk.)
    1. Copyright--United States--Popular works.   I. Title.
KF2995.B47   1997
346.7304'82--dc21   96-53388
                                                                      CIP

To my father, Gene G., who shared with me early in my life his love for intellectual property.

Acknowledgments

When Wendy Keller of ForthWrite Literary Agency called and asked if I had ever considered writing a book on copyright, I immediately said yes. Of course I had considered writing a book, but instead had decided to publish a newsletter—*copyRights©*—which was what she had in her hands and the reason for her call. Wendy convinced me of something I already knew: In addition to the newsletter, there needed to be a book on the subject. When she called in January 1996, I had no idea I would really write the book, but here it is. Thank you, Wendy.

It has been said that we are the sum total of all our life experiences. As we go through life it is these experiences that shape our thoughts, words and actions. With that in mind, *Copyright Plain and Simple* could not have been written without the help and inspiration of many experiences and special people.

In gratitude, I would like to thank Barbara Bartolotta and Robert Ravas, my mentors at ScottForesman; The Permissions Group—Sherry, Lin, Stephanie, Joe, Jean and Mary Ann—for their neverending enthusiasm and constant willingness to roll up their sleeves and meet all our challenges; my parents Ruth and Gene Gross and my Aunt Marge and Uncle Jack Romano for believing in me and Joe when we wanted to start our company (Although my Dad and Jack are no longer with us, their presence continues to be felt every day.); my grown sons Roger and Brian who always show interest in my life even though they are far and away; to my daughter Kate who has grown up in the "board room" of The Permissions Group; and special thanks to my best friend and husband, Joe, who continues to be one of my greatest life experiences and is my partner in all that I do.

Copyright Plain and Simple would not have been set in type if it weren't for the support and encouragement of many. Special thanks to Wendy Keller of ForthWrite Literary Agency for encouraging me to stretch myself and my time; to Ron Fry at Career Press for believing in the project from the beginning; to Laura N. Gasaway, director of the law library and professor of law at the University of North Carolina, for her ongoing assistance with *copyRights©* without which this book would not exist; to Professor James S. Heller, director of the law library and professor of law at The College of William and Mary, for lending his legal eye to the manuscript; and to my editors at Career Press, Betsy Sheldon, Ellen Scher, Regina McAloney and Suzanne Gruber, who have massaged my words and brought this book to publication.

Contents

Preface

Ever since I started my copyright consulting company, a number of people have asked me the same question: "Is there a really good book on copyright?" Until the publication of this book, I didn't have a good answer for them. Not because there weren't any books with useful information on copyright. Because there are several.

But I knew what these folks were really looking for. Most of them had a number of basic questions about copyright. The majority of the books had more information than the average copyright consultant needed to know (or any attorney for that matter) about the subject.

These people had questions like, "How do I get a copyright for my poem?" "If something is really old it's in the public domain, right?" "How do I get permission to use copyright-protected material and when do I need to get it?" "If I change the words a little, is it fair use?" "What *is* fair use?"

The fact was, there were no "really good books on copyright." Not the kind these folks were looking for—something that would speak to their everyday questions.

Enter Wendy Keller of ForthWrite Literary Agency. Wendy had seen a copy of my newsletter called *copy-Rights*© and was wondering if I had ever considered writing a book. I told her I had, but that I was so busy with my rights and permissions consulting company and the newsletter, the book would have to wait a few years.

After she and I discussed the matter for a while and I related all the requests I had received for the "really good book on copyright," Wendy finally convinced me that sooner was better than later, and that giving one more job to a busy person was one of the best ways to get it done.

As I put together my vision for *Copyright Plain and Simple,* I recalled one of those "life experiences" I spoke of in the acknowledgments. My husband, Joe, had had the opportunity to see the Reverend Jesse Jackson speak at Operation PUSH in Chicago. As Rev. Jackson delivered his message, Joe was taken by one phrase that some members of the audience shouted out during Jackson's speech: "Make it plain, Jesse. Make it plain." As this book was taking shape, this phrase continued to resonate in my mind. And I knew that I was being called upon to "make it plain."

The electronic age has made us all creators and users of copyright material—whether we realize it or not. Whether you are a college student honing your computer skills by creating a home page on the World Wide Web, a freelance desktop publisher building your business or a songwriter creating digital music, you definitely have a need to know about copyright. The mission of *Copyright Plain and Simple* is to make copyright plain—to take the law, boil it down, and apply it to our everyday lives through everyday examples.

And although my goal is to simplify the law for you, the truth is that the law can be complex and each copyright situation can bring its own unique set of circumstances. I believe that *Copyright Plain and Simple* will serve as a valuable resource for explaining copyright basics, answering everyday questions and providing a springboard when your copyright situation goes beyond plain and simple.

―――――

The Congress shall have Power...To Promote the
Progress of Science and useful Arts, by securing for
limited Times to Authors and Inventors the
exclusive Right to their respective Writings
and Discoveries...

—Article 1, Section 8, U.S. Constitution

1

Copyright
Affects Everyone

You've found some photos of your relatives from long ago in an old trunk in the attic. Time and the elements have taken their toll, but you have heard of a new technology that can restore old photos. You're thrilled to think that these lost treasures can soon be adorning your mantel. You bring them to the local camera shop.

The gentleman behind the counter tells you he'll be happy to restore your photos. He shows you the equipment and gives you a demonstration of the process. Then he asks you the most peculiar question: Do you have written permission to reproduce the photos?

Why would you need permission? They're your photos! You explain that these are pictures of your family members taken more than 100 years ago. He says that before he can process the photos you'll need to have proof in writing that you have permission to reproduce them. "From whom?" you ask; all these relatives are long-departed. He tells you to find the studio that took the pictures and get written permission. He politely explains that the copyright law forbids the reproduction of photos without permission. How can this be?

❖ ❖ ❖ ❖

You are a high school student learning to construct home pages on the World Wide Web. You decide that a local paper has a great guide to the town's night life, which everyone should have access to. You go to great lengths to recreate the guide and "link" it to other pages with similar themes. You make sure to let other "net surfers" know that you got the information from your hometown paper. You're so proud of your new creation that you write to the paper about what you've done, expecting to receive a thank-you letter because you've provided them with some free advertising. Instead of kudos, you receive a letter requesting you remove the page you've created, as well as something about "theft of information" and "copyright infringement."

❖ ❖ ❖ ❖

You are the vice-president of marketing in an accounting firm. You are preparing a slide presentation to be shown to prospective clients during a series of meetings you will be holding at a national convention. You want to include music—in particular, you want to use the first five seconds of the *Dragnet* theme. Your production coordinator asks if the budget allows for the fee involved in using the song cut. You are surprised by his comment. He tells you what he paid for the use of the five seconds for another project. You had no idea that such a small cut needed permission, much less an exorbitant fee.

Copyright affects everyone

You may not be one of the chosen few who know the formula for Coca-Cola® (trade secret), or invented a cardio-vascular exercise machine that revolutionizes the fitness industry (patent), or created a multibillion dollar company with a burger and two yellow arches (trademark). But anyone who has ever written a letter, snapped a photo, painted a picture, whittled a bird on the end of a walking stick, taped a favorite show from television, or sung "Happy Birthday" at a party is involved in copyright.

Today, with home computers in some 40 percent of U.S. households, anyone can be a desktop publisher. Whether we are creating a newsletter for a scout troop, collecting all our mother's favorite recipes to be bound as a family gift, designing greeting cards to be sold at a Christmas boutique, or writing a book on copyright— copyright is indeed part of our everyday lives.

Copyright is big business. The International Intellectual Property Alliance reports, "The copyright industries contribute more to the U.S. economy and employ more workers than any single manufacturing sector including aircraft, primary metals, textiles, apparel, or chemicals." According to the report, in 1993 the U.S. copyright industry achieved foreign sales of $45.8 billion, making it the "second-largest industry in exports and foreign sales after automobiles and parts."

The U.S. government has exhibited an understanding of the importance of copyright in the electronic age. In February 1993 President Clinton formed the Information Infrastructure Task Force to study the impact of the National Information Infrastructure (otherwise known as the electronic superhighway) and to update the law on copyright if necessary. The Working Group on Intellectual Property Rights published its findings in a white paper, "Intellectual Property and the National Information Infrastructure," in September 1995. With this paper in hand, our legislators have been debating legislation regarding the current and future needs of this nation in protecting copyrighted material while encouraging the creativity that moves us forward.

Yet ask the average person on the street what copyright is and you get a response such as, "It's that little 'c' thing with a circle that means somebody owns it." Most citizens do not understand copyright or why we would need to protect it.

Perhaps this example will hit home: What if you returned from work one day and found that the maple tree in your front yard had been cut down? Or that your furniture was rearranged—nothing missing—just rearranged? What if someone set up a tent on your front lawn? After you recovered from the shock, you would probably take immediate steps to protect your property. You might ask the people to get off your property or call the police.

We all understand the concept of "real" (as in real estate) property. There are laws to protect "real" property—no one has the right to trespass. The same is true for "intellectual" property. No one has the right to trespass on it. This right is granted in the Copyright Act of 1976, the current copyright law.

Copyright knowledge is important

We would like to think that *piracy* only took place on the high seas in days gone by. Yet millions of revenue dollars are lost through piracy of copyrighted material every year. And what about *cyber*-piracy? This new word in the English language is getting a lot of notoriety. Senator Orrin G. Hatch (R-Utah) has proposed bills to protect copyrighted material on the Internet. He states that "no manufacturer would ship his or her goods on a highway if his trucks were routinely hijacked."

If creators of copyrighted material ("manufacturers") are routinely "hijacked," these creators might no longer be encouraged to create. This could hinder the goal of copyright granted in the Constitution of the United States to "promote the progress of science and useful arts." Respect for the property is important for our country to move forward intellectually and creatively.

If you are a creator of copyrighted material, it is important to understand your rights. We are on the brink of an even newer technological dawn. Information is sent or received around the world with one stroke of a computer key. Old photos can look as though they were taken yesterday. Any student doing a research paper can type "Maya Angelou" on a search of the Internet and download her poem, "On the Pulse of Morning," written for and recited at President Clinton's inauguration.

We are able to dabble with other people's intellectual property so easily we may not even consider that the property is protected, that there is an invisible "no trespassing" sign on it or a fence around it.

It is everyone's responsibility to know the law and understand the way it is applied in all media so that we can make responsible and intelligent decisions about the way we use other people's property.

The cost for *not* understanding copyright protection could be high. Just ask George Frena. In 1993, Playboy Enterprises sued cybervendor Frena for transmitting digitized images of Playboy photographs. Although Frena removed the images whenever his customers transmitted them onto his system, a court found Frena liable for infringing on Playboy's copyrights and trademarks. ("Playboy" and "Playmate" are registered trademarks.) Even though these were instances of "innocent" infringement, nonetheless, Frena was liable.

It is essential to fully understand the copyright law and its application to our real lives—as we sit down to write that term paper, or create "Grandma's Best Recipes" or take in our photos to be restored. Use *Copyright Plain and Simple* to make a sometimes complex law understandable. Then you can go to the camera store employee and tell him that because your family photos were "published" more than 75 years ago, they are out of copyright and in the public domain. Permission is no longer needed from the studio (if the studio was indeed the copyright holder) and the photos are free for anyone to use and reproduce.

A look at what you'll learn

You come into contact with copyright law much more often than you realize. Whether you're writing a book or creating your church bulletin, you're involved in copyright. Here's a brief overview of the issues we'll explore in *Copyright Plain and Simple*:

♦ What is copyright and why is it important?

♦ What is an "intellectual property" and how is it similar to other types of property?

♦ When did copyright law start, and how has it changed over the years?

♦ What types of properties are protected by copyright, and what types aren't?

♦ How are books, magazines, and other forms of the printed word protected by copyright?

♦ Does copyright for visual works of art such as paintings and photographs differ from other types of copyright?

♦ Can a performance such as a play, a ballet, or a speech be protected by copyright?

♦ Can you make a copy of a CD you bought to play in your car? What if you want to make a copy for a friend? What copyright issues are important when it comes to music?

♦ How has copyright changed with the boom in computer technology?

♦ You noticed a sign about copyright at your local copy shop. What do you need to know about copyright and photocopying?

♦ How do you know who holds the rights to an intellectual property? And how do you get permission to use it?

♦ What is "fair use" and when can you claim it?

♦ What constitutes copyright infringement and how can you avoid it?

♦ What special copyright concerns do libraries and educational institutions face?

♦ With all the changes in technology, what does the future hold for copyright law?

Whether you are dealing with the printed word, visual arts, music, film, the theater, or software, this book will give you practical applications of the law. It will help you to protect your own intellectual properties, as well as minimize your risk of liability when using properties that belong to others. Whether you start here and read to the end, or start with the section that most applies to your own unique situation, this book will be an invaluable guide that explains copyright *plain and simple*.

2

What Is Copyright?

If you came home from work one day and found that your prize rose bushes had been cut to the ground or your garage door was sporting a new coat of pink latex, you would be on the phone to the police as soon as you could say "no trespassing!!"

Real vs. intellectual property

We are all aware of our rights as "real" property owners. No one has the right to come onto our property and, certainly, no one has the right to deface or destroy it. There are laws to protect our property—and we know our rights!

But let's say that you have written an historical novel based on the life and times of Napoleon Bonaparte. Soon after your novel is published you see a movie on HBO that bears a striking resemblance to your work. You should be on the phone to an attorney as fast as you can say "derivative work!!"

Both real property and intellectual property have much in common. Intellectual property may not be something you can put your arms around, but it exists and it has value. Time and effort may have gone into the creating and shaping of it. No one should have the right to trespass on or deface it. Just as real property is protected by law, so is intellectual property protected by law—*copyright* law.

Copyright roots

The foundations for U.S. copyright law were laid down more than 300 years ago in England. With the advent and popularity of printing technology, the intellectual property of others became more accessible. Before the printing press, the *pirating* of another's work required the investment of a great deal of time and effort. Was it worth it? All that time and effort to make one copy?

The new technology of the printing press raised new issues. Now an author's work could be reproduced quickly and at much less expense—which meant a greater audience and greater revenue—for *someone*. Paul Goldstein, in his book *Copyright's Highway,* addresses the issues this new technology raised:

> *"Who should be entitled to share in the newly opened cache of literary value? The author who created the text? The publisher who financed the risk that copies of the text might never find enough readers to repay the cost of printing and distributing it? Or—once author and publisher were paid—the public, in the form of lower prices?"[1]*

In 1557, 80 years after William Caxton brought the printing press to England, a royal charter was granted to a guild of scribes, printers, bookbinders and booksellers. For the next few hundred years, the Stationers' Company

---

[1] Paul Goldstein, *Copyright's Highway.* New York: Hill and Wang, 1994, p. 40.

controlled the rights to writings. These rights were passed down through the generations, in perpetuity. Writers were paid lump sums for their work and had no rights. The Stationers' Company had a monopoly on the publishing business. It was truly an era of "publisher's rights."

The Statute of Anne

The Crown of England was anxious to control the words that came off the press. A variety of censorship acts led to the Licensing Act of 1662. This act originally had a two-year term but was renewed continually.

Resentment mounted regarding the monopoly and powers of censorship of the Stationer's Company. In 1709, this monopoly was broken when Parliament refused to renew the Licensing Act of 1662 and with the enactment of the Statute of Anne. No longer was it a violation of the stationers' copyright to publish a work.

The Statute of Anne was written as an "Act for the encouragement of learning, by vesting the copies of printed books in the authors or purchasers of such copies, during the times therein mentioned." The statute provided copyright protection to the author for a term of 28 years. Thus began the period of "author's rights."

First U.S. Law, 1790

The Statute of Anne, carried across the Atlantic Ocean by early English colonists, underwent testing and evolution that continued after the colonies won independence from England. As a result of lobbying by writers such as Noah Webster and Thomas Paine, its concepts were incorporated into early state copyright laws.

The U.S. Congress articulated its idea of copyright by using the following language: "The Congress shall have power...to promote the progress of science and useful arts, by securing for limited times to authors and inventors the exclusive right to their respective writings and discoveries." On May 31, 1790, President George Washington signed into effect the first national Copyright Act, granting a 14-year term of copyright protection for books, maps, and charts. On June 9, 1790 the first copyrighted work was registered in the U.S. District Court of Pennsylvania—*The Philadelphia Spelling Book* by John Barry.

The Copyright Act of 1909

Over the years other technologies have tested and changed the U.S. law. Music gained copyright protection in 1831, dramatic compositions were added in 1856, and photography became copyrightable in 1865, presumably due to Mathew Brady, the famous Civil War photographer.

It was the player piano that brought about a significant change in the law. Apollo, a manufacturer of player pianos, was sued by White-Smith Music Publishing Co. for copyright infringement in 1908. Although printed music was protected by copyright, recorded music was not. Player pianos posed the question—Was paper with holes a "copy" of musical notation? Composers Victor Herbert and John Philip Sousa testified in favor of protection. It seemed evident that the law needed changing. The copyright law was revised and the Copyright Act of 1909 was enacted.

The Copyright Act of 1976

The first 70 years of the 20th century has been called the Era of Communications. The phonograph, radio, television, photocopier, video camera, and computers were all introduced during this time. Until the late 1970s, copyright law only protected those works that were *published*— publication being defined as the distribution of copies of a work to the public by sale or other transfer of ownership, or by rental, lease, or lending. The offering to distribute copies of a work to a group of people for the purposes of further distribution, public performance, or public display also constitutes publication.

William S. Strong, in his book *The Copyright Book: A Practical Guide,* interprets the legal definition of publication:

> *"The concept of publication has been crucial to copyright law from the beginning. Publication is the act of offering copies to the public. There does not have to be an actual distribution. Even if there is a distribution, it does not have to be a sale; giving copies away to the public is sufficient. The size of the public is irrelevant; handing out one or two copies can constitute publication. And though performance or display of a work is not publication in and of itself, distributing copies to a group of persons who will themselves perform or display the work does not count as publication, unless those persons are your employees or otherwise act under your control."[2]*

In 1976, revisions were proposed that meant that creators no longer needed to publish a work for it to be copyrighted. Copyright was immediate—at creation. Thus began an era of greater author's rights. This revision was enacted January 1, 1978 although the name of the act remains the Copyright Act of 1976. It is still our current law for the protection of copyrighted property.

What is copyrightable?

Copyright law lists the following types of works of authorship as those that can be protected by copyright:

♦ Literary works.

♦ Musical works, including any accompanying words.

---

2 William S. Strong, *The Copyright Book: A Practical Guide, Fourth Edition.* Cambridge, Mass.: The MIT Press, 1994, p. 78.

- Dramatic works, including any accompanying music.
- Pantomimes and choreographic works.
- Pictorial, graphic, and sculptural works.
- Motion pictures and other audiovisual works.
- Sound recordings.
- Architectural works.

What is not copyrightable?

The following are *not* protected by copyright law in the United States. While some may be protected by trademark or patent law or possibly by laws prohibiting unfair competition, they are not copyrightable.

- Works that are not in a fixed form of expression. For example, choreographic works that have not been notated or recorded, extemporaneous speech or improvisational performances that are not written or recorded.
- Titles, names, short phrases, and slogans (these may be protected by trademark law).
- Familiar symbols or designs—such as "smiley faces" and no-smoking signs.
- Type fonts, lettering, or coloring.
- Ideas, procedures, methods, systems, processes, concepts, principles, discoveries, or devices.
- Works consisting entirely of information that is common property and containing no original authorship. For example: standard calendars, height and weight charts, tape measures and rulers, lists or tables taken from public documents or other common sources.

The requirements of copyright

Copyright protection is awarded to works of authorship that are:

- ◆ Original.
- ◆ Exhibit minimal creativity.
- ◆ Fixed in a tangible form of expression. Fixed form is defined as a form that can preserve the work so that it can be read back or heard, either directly or with the aid of a machine.

The more creative the work, and the more you can prove your work is unique, the more likely your work will be granted protection. Start with a stick figure drawing and there may not be much to copyright. But add a plaid scarf, a beret and give the figure a name and you are on your way to creating a copyrightable character.

What are the *exclusive rights* granted by law to copyrighted works? According to Section 106 of Title 17 of the United States Code, the following rights in copyrighted works are protected. The copyright owner has the *exclusive rights* to and authorizes others to:

- ◆ Reproduce the work.
- ◆ Prepare derivative works of the work.
- ◆ Distribute copies of the work.
- ◆ Perform the work publicly.
- ◆ Display the work publicly.

What is a reproduction?

One of the exclusive rights of a copyright holder is the right to make copies of or reproduce a protected work. Here are examples of reproductions of copyrighted works:

- A photocopy of a magazine article.
- An extra set of prints from your roll of film.
- A photograph that has been scanned into a computer.
- A print copy of an electronic mail message.
- A copy of a cassette.
- A backup of a computer disk.

What is a derivative work?

The copyright owner has the exclusive right to create adaptations of a protected work and transform the protected work into a new work. The following are examples of derivative works:

- A screenplay from a novel.
- A painting from a photo.
- A postcard from a painting.
- A rap song from a rock song.
- A puzzle created from a photo.
- A fabric pattern from a graphic design.
- A ballad from a poem.

What is distribution?

The following are examples of ways in which a copyrighted work might be distributed.

- Passing out pamphlets on a street corner.
- Sending an article to clients.
- Publishing and selling a book throughout the world.

- Sending an electronic message to another person in a company.
- Displaying brochures in a rack on a store counter.
- Mailing a flyer to residents in a particular area.

What is a public performance?

Public performance of a copyrighted work is another right that the copyright owner holds. Here are a few examples of performances:

- Acting on a stage.
- Singing in a club.
- Making a recording.
- Showing a movie in a theater.
- Broadcasting a sports event.

What is a public display?

A copyright holder has the exclusive right to publicly display a copyrighted work. Here are some examples protected by copyright law:

- Posting the work on a bulletin board.
- Hanging a print on the wall of a library.
- Displaying the work on a classroom computer screen.
- Exhibiting a painting at an art gallery.
- Placing a sculpture in the lobby of a building.

Two important concepts to remember

1. Ideas are not copyrightable! The idea "four-bedroom house" can mean different things to different people.

That idea is not copyrightable. What is copyrightable is the *expression* of the idea "four-bedroom house." The architect designs the floor plans for the house, a writer describes the house in a short story, a photographer captures the house in the late-afternoon sun, a painter renders a water-color likeness, a lyricist writes a ballad about the house—and so on. Each artist has portrayed the idea "four-bedroom house" through a different form of expression. It is this expression, this unique way of expressing the idea, that is copyrightable.

2. Facts are not copyrightable! You are driving to the coffee shop down the street. You see a car swerve off the road, hit a fence, and knock down a mailbox. You stop your car check on the driver who appears to have some minor cuts and bruises but is in good spirits. Speaking of spirits, you do smell alcohol. As you call the police department on your cell phone to report this, you note that your watch says it is 1:30 p.m. The facts in this sequence of events are not copyrightable in and of themselves. But a news story about the events written by a reporter for the local paper *is* copyrightable. In other words, neither you nor anyone else has the exclusive right to tell the story about the incident. But once the story is told—by the news reporter or TV commentator—that expression of the story as related by the reporter or commentator is protected by copyright.

Transferring copyright

Just as with any real property, any or all of the exclusive rights—and any subdivision of those rights—involving an intellectual property can be bought, sold, and transferred. The homeowner can sell his home, rent it, donate it to an organization, or will it to his children. So can the artist transfer his intellectual property; sell it, rent it, donate it to an organization, or will it to his children.

Because these rights are exclusive to the owner, the transfer must be conveyed by contractual agreement—in writing. You wouldn't think of letting someone rent your house for a year without a lease. What if the tenants burned a hole in the carpeting? What if they had 10 friends move in right away? What if they never made their payments? Just as with real property, it is important to spell out (in writing) all expectations and restrictions regarding intellectual property.

Types of transfers

Transfers of any or all rights in an author's copyright should not be taken lightly. It is a contractual arrangement. The following are types of transfers:

1. Exclusive license—a transfer of one or more of the rights of a copyright holder.
2. Nonexclusive license—allowing someone the right to exercise one or more of the rights on a nonexclusive basis. This is not a transfer of copyright ownership.
3. Assignment—a transfer of all the exclusive rights in a copyright.

A transfer of copyright ownership must be in writing to be valid. It is also a good idea to record an all-rights transfer, an *assignment*, with the Copyright Office. The assignment is then a matter of public record. The process is similar to recording a deed with the county in which you reside.

What are subsidiary rights?

As mentioned earlier, your property can be *subdivided*. The rights that protect portions of the property are called subsidiary rights.

An example of subsidiary rights can be found in virtually any book-publishing contract between an author and publisher. The primary right in a literary work is the right of publication. When an author signs a contract, he or she is granting to the publisher the right to print copies of the work and distribute the copies to be sold. All other rights are the subsidiary rights. These can include:

♦ Printing of paperback editions (or hardbound editions if the contract is for paperback).

♦ Selling the work to be made into a movie, TV show, play, or radio series.

♦ Publishing all or part of the work in a newspaper, magazine, or other periodical.

♦ Making or selling foreign translations of the work.

♦ Making audio recordings of a literary work (a book or poem).

♦ Electronic rights.

Subsidiary rights are negotiable and valuable. If you have written a book, for example, you may want to retain all rights for foreign translations, audio recordings, or electronic rights of your work. Be sure you understand what rights you have, what rights you want, and what rights you are willing to give away.

What is a work for hire?

When is the creator of an intellectual property *not* the owner of the copyright? When the work is created in a work-for-hire situation. Although the Copyright Act of 1976 states that copyright protection begins at creation and when a work is in a fixed form, it also defines two situations in which the creator of a work does not have the rights to the work.

The first situation is when an employee performs or creates work for his or her employer within the scope of the employee's job description. This is an understood agreement between the two parties and no agreement in writing is necessary. What constitutes a work made by an employee? It is the kind of work the employee is asked to perform. It occurs during the employee's work hours. It is performed to serve the employer.

For example, a copy writer for an ad agency is hired to write text for advertising. Therefore, if that employee creates a brochure while working there, it is the agency's right to profit from that work—not the creator of the brochure.

The other situation in which the creator does not have the copyright protection is when the work is considered a work for hire. When a company or individual commissions work by an author, copyright ownership clearly rests with the commissioning party if the agreement between the two parties is in writing. The following are types of commissioned works that are considered to be works for hire under the Copyright Act of 1976.

♦ A contribution to a collective work.

♦ Part of a motion picture or other audiovisual work, such as a screenplay.

♦ A translation.

♦ A supplementary work prepared as an adjunct to a work prepared by another person, such as a foreword, index, appendix, chart, illustration, map, or bibliography.

♦ A compilation.

♦ An instructional text.

♦ A test or answer key.

♦ An atlas.

Who is the author in a work-for-hire situation? For copyright purposes, the employer or the party who commissions the work is the author of the work and, thus, the copyright holder. This copyright holder can be a person or an entity, such as a company.

Important!! In order to be valid, a work-for-hire agreement should be signed before the work begins.

Negotiating a contract

Whether you are writing the great American novel, creating an index for a textbook, or drawing a cartoon strip for your local paper, it is essential that you understand your rights. Before signing any contractual agreement, understand what you are keeping or giving away. A good resource for understanding publishing law is *Kirsch's Handbook of Publishing Law* by Jonathan Kirsch (See Appendix A). If you are not sure about the language, have an attorney review your contract. You could be giving away valuable rights!

Edgar Rice Burroughs, the creator of Tarzan, clearly understood the importance of property rights. In his article "Protecting the Author's Rights," which he wrote for *The Writers 1932 Year Book & Market Guide,* he cautioned authors: "Watch all of your rights all of the time; they are the basis of your entire literary estate." Your property (be it real or intellectual) has great value. Enjoy the protection you are granted under the law.

Summary

Copyright protects intellectual property, just as other laws protect real property. Pertinent parts of the Copyright Act are reprinted in Appendix C in this book. In the meantime, here are some highlights regarding the origins and foundations of copyright law:

♦ U.S. copyright law began even before there was a U.S.—with the Statute of Anne in England in 1709.

♦ The U.S. copyright law is founded in the Constitution, Article I, Section 8.

♦ The first U.S. Copyright Act was signed into law by George Washington on May 31, 1790.

♦ The next major change in copyright came with the Copyright Act of 1909, as a result of an infringement suit over player pianos.

♦ The Copyright Act of 1976 is the current copyright law that governs us.

♦ Current copyright law grants a copyright holder the following exclusive rights:
  1. The right to reproduce the work.
  2. The right to prepare derivative works.
  3. The right to distribute copies of the work.
  4. The right to perform the work publicly.
  5. The right to display the work publicly.

♦ It is the buying and selling of these rights that give intellectual property economic value.

♦ Ideas are not copyrightable.

♦ Facts are not copyrightable.

♦ When negotiating a contract that involves copyright issues, be aware of the rights you are keeping and those you are selling (or giving away!).

3

Copyright
Basics

Despite the title of this people, most people don't think of copyright as simple. In fact, copyright can be quite perplexing. If you learn the basics, though, you will have the tools to view each copyright situation appropriately and apply a foundation of knowledge to find the answers you need.

Old law and new law

As we touched on in the previous chapter, you need to be familiar with the two U.S. copyright laws: the Copyright Act of 1909 and the current law, the Copyright Act of 1976.

Why is it important to be familiar with the old act? While you are creating works under the current law, you may very well want to use works created under the old law. The current law became effective on January 1, 1978. For copyright purposes we will discuss works as having been created before 1978 or after 1978. The two laws are significantly different. One of the first questions you must ask yourself when considering use of others' material is, "What law was it created/published under?"

The Copyright Act of 1909

Under the Copyright Act of 1909, a work had to be *published* to be awarded copyright protection. In addition, the work had to have a notice of copyright, and the copyright had to have been registered. If the work was published without a valid copyright notice, it fell into the public domain. The initial term of copyright was 28 years. Copyright could be renewed for an additional term of 28 years. When the current law came into effect, the renewal term of previous copyrights was extended an additional 19 years. For this reason, the full term of copyright protection for works published under the Copyright Act of 1909 was 75 years. In summary, here are the highlights of the old law:

♦ Publication was required for copyright protection.

♦ The law provided a 28-year term with a 28-year renewal term.

♦ A valid copyright notice had to appear with the work.

♦ The copyright had to be registered.

The Copyright Act of 1976

Under the current law, copyright protection is immediate and begins at the creation of an original work of authorship in a fixed, tangible means of expression.

The current Copyright Act redefines the terms of protection, as well. A single term of copyright is defined as either of the following:

♦ Life of the author plus 50 years for a work by an individual author or authors.

♦ 75 years from creation or 100 years from publication, whichever is sooner, for a company.

A copyright notice was a requirement of the Copyright Act of 1976 until March 1, 1989 when the United States adhered to the Berne Convention of International Copyright, which eliminated the need for a copyright notice as a requirement for protection. Before that time, works published without a copyright notice were not granted copyright protection under the law—and they entered the public domain. A creator of an intellectual property could correct this error of omission if he or she registered the work and made a reasonable effort to add a valid notice of copyright to all copies distributed after the omission was discovered.

Copyright registration is optional, although very desirable, entitling the copyright holder to statutory damages and attorney fees should the holder prove copyright infringement. Before a copyright suit can begin, the copyright holder must prove a valid copyright in the work by registering the work with the Copyright Office and receiving a recorded certificate of copyright registration. While copyright protection is granted by law at creation and fixation and a copyright owner does have the right to tell an infringer to stop using the work, the holder *must* bring to court this "deed" to the property—the certificate of registration.

To summarize, here are the highlights of the Copyright Act of 1976:

♦ Creation in fixed form is the key to protection.

♦ A single term of copyright—life of the author and 50 years for individuals, or 75 years from publication or 100 years from creation, whichever is first, for a company.

♦ Notice of copyright is optional after March 1, 1989.

♦ Registration of copyright is optional, although highly desirable.

Copyright renewal

Issues of renewal apply only to copyrights established prior to the enactment of the current law in 1978. Under the previous act, at the end of the first copyright term of 28 years, the copyright holder had until the 28th year of the term to submit a renewal application to the Copyright Office in order to receive another term. If the application was not received by December 31 of that year, the copyright for the work expired and the work fell into public domain. Copyright could not be recaptured.

The law was amended in 1992 to provide an automatic renewal of copyrights. It had been discovered that only 20 percent of copyrights were renewed. This means that it can be assumed that any works published before 1964 have a 28-year term and a 47-year renewal period if a timely filing of renewal was done. After 1964, published works have full 75 year protection.

Unpublished works

Until the Copyright Act of 1976 unpublished works were protected under common-law copyright and subject to state rather than federal law. A special provision in the new law, which protects a work at creation rather than at publication, protects works of original authorship that were unpublished before 1978 until December 31, 2002. If the work was published between January 1, 1978 and January 1, 2003, the copyright of the work cannot expire before December 31, 2027. In other words, you can get an extension of protection of an additional 25 years.

Copyright registration

Although the first copyright law was enacted in 1790, it was not until 1870 that the copyright functions were centralized under the Library of Congress. Until that time, registrations of copyright were recorded by clerks of U.S. District Courts. As of fiscal year 1995, more than 26 million works had been registered with the Library of Congress. In 1995 alone, more than 609,195 claims were registered.

When works pass into the public domain

Date of work	Protected from	Term
Created 1/1/78 or after	When work is fixed in tangible medium of expression	Life + 50 years (or, if work of corporate authorship, 75 years from publication, or 100 years from creation, whichever is first)
Published more than 75 years ago	Now in public domain	None
Published between 1963 and 75 years ago	When published with notice	28 years + could be renewed for 47 years; if not so renewed, now in public domain
Published 1964-1977	When published with notice	28 years for first term; now automatic extension of 47 years for second term
Created before 1/1/78 but not published	1/1/78, the effective date of the 1976 Act which eliminated common law copyright	Life + 50 years of 12/31/2002, whichever is greater
Created before 1/1/78 but published between then and 12/31/2002	1/1/78, the effective date of the Act which eliminated common law copyright	Passes into public domain 12/31/2027

http://www.lib.umich.edu/libhome/copyright/chart.html
Prepared by Laura N. Gasaway, Professor of Law, University of North Carolina

What is involved in registering your copyrighted work? The following items must be submitted in the same package to the Copyright Office (Register of Copyrights, Library of Congress, Washington, DC 20559):

- A completed registration form.
- Two copies of the "best edition" of your work.
- A $20 filing fee per registration.

Why register a work? As mentioned earlier, it is a prerequisite to an infringement suit. Registration must be made in a timely fashion—within three months of the date of the first publication or before the date the copyright infringement began. For unpublished works a copyright owner is entitled to statutory damages and attorney fees from the perpetrator only if the work was registered before the infringement occurred. If you find yourself in a hurry to register your work before a suit, the expedited registration will cost an additional $200.

Anyone who has questions may call the Copyright Public Information Office at 202-707-3000 for recorded information. Information specialists can answer questions by phone or in person Monday through Friday, 8:30 a.m. to 5 p.m., except federal holidays.

The Copyright Office Forms Hotline number is available 24 hours a day to accept requests for specific registration application forms and for information circulars. Call 202-707-9100. Address written inquiries to Publication Section, LM-455, Copyright Office, Library of Congress, Washington, DC 20559-6000.

Registration forms

Following are some of the types of registration forms to be completed. When in doubt as to what form to use, speak with an information specialist at the Copyright Office.

- **TX—Nondramatic Literary Works.** This form is used for works such as books, articles, computer programs, databases, speeches, poems, and essays.

FORM TX
For a Literary Work
UNITED STATES COPYRIGHT OFFICE

REGISTRATION NUMBER

_____
TX   TXU
EFFECTIVE DATE OF REGISTRATION

_____
Month   Day   Year

DO NOT WRITE ABOVE THIS LINE. IF YOU NEED MORE SPACE, USE A SEPARATE CONTINUATION SHEET.

TITLE OF THIS WORK ▼

PREVIOUS OR ALTERNATIVE TITLES ▼

PUBLICATION AS A CONTRIBUTION If this work was published as a contribution to a periodical, serial, or collection, give information about the collective work in which the contribution appeared.   **Title of Collective Work ▼**

If published in a periodical or serial give: **Volume ▼**   **Number ▼**   **Issue Date ▼**   **On Pages ▼**

2

a

NAME OF AUTHOR ▼

DATES OF BIRTH AND DEATH
Year Born ▼   Year Died ▼

Was this contribution to the work a "work made for hire"?
☐ Yes
☐ No

AUTHOR'S NATIONALITY OR DOMICILE
Name of Country
OR { Citizen of ▶
Domiciled in▶

WAS THIS AUTHOR'S CONTRIBUTION TO THE WORK
Anonymous?   ☐ Yes ☐ No
Pseudonymous? ☐ Yes ☐ No
If the answer to either of these questions is "Yes," see detailed instructions.

NATURE OF AUTHORSHIP Briefly describe nature of material created by this author in which copyright is claimed. ▼

b

NAME OF AUTHOR ▼

DATES OF BIRTH AND DEATH
Year Born ▼   Year Died ▼

Was this contribution to the work a "work made for hire"?
☐ Yes
☐ No

AUTHOR'S NATIONALITY OR DOMICILE
Name of Country
OR { Citizen of ▶
Domiciled in▶

WAS THIS AUTHOR'S CONTRIBUTION TO THE WORK
Anonymous?   ☐ Yes ☐ No
Pseudonymous? ☐ Yes ☐ No
If the answer to either of these questions is "Yes," see detailed instructions.

NATURE OF AUTHORSHIP Briefly describe nature of material created by this author in which copyright is claimed. ▼

c

NAME OF AUTHOR ▼

DATES OF BIRTH AND DEATH
Year Born ▼   Year Died ▼

Was this contribution to the work a "work made for hire"?
☐ Yes
☐ No

AUTHOR'S NATIONALITY OR DOMICILE
Name of Country
OR { Citizen of ▶
Domiciled in▶

WAS THIS AUTHOR'S CONTRIBUTION TO THE WORK
Anonymous?   ☐ Yes ☐ No
Pseudonymous? ☐ Yes ☐ No
If the answer to either of these questions is "Yes," see detailed instructions.

NATURE OF AUTHORSHIP Briefly describe nature of material created by this author in which copyright is claimed. ▼

3

a **YEAR IN WHICH CREATION OF THIS WORK WAS COMPLETED** This information must be given ◀Year in all cases.

b **DATE AND NATION OF FIRST PUBLICATION OF THIS PARTICULAR WORK** Complete this information ONLY if this work has been published.   Month ▶ _____ Day▶ _____ Year ▶ _____   ◀ Nation

---

4

COPYRIGHT CLAIMANT(S) Name and address must be given even if the claimant is the same as the author given in space 2. ▼

TRANSFER If the claimant(s) named here in space 4 is (are) different from the author(s) named in space 2, give a brief statement of how the claimant(s) obtained ownership of the copyright. ▼

APPLICATION RECEIVED

ONE DEPOSIT RECEIVED

TWO DEPOSITS RECEIVED

FUNDS RECEIVED

DO NOT WRITE HERE OFFICE USE ONLY

MORE ON BACK ▶ • Complete all applicable spaces (numbers 5-11) on the reverse side of this page.
• See detailed instructions.   • Sign the form at line 10.

DO NOT WRITE HERE
Page 1 of _____ pages

Copyright Plain and Simple

EXAMINED BY _____

CHECKED BY _____

☐ CORRESPONDENCE
☐ Yes

FORM T

FOR
COPYRIG
OFFICE
USE
ONLY

DO NOT WRITE ABOVE THIS LINE. IF YOU NEED MORE SPACE, USE A SEPARATE CONTINUATION SHEET.

PREVIOUS REGISTRATION Has registration for this work, or for an earlier version of this work, already been made in the Copyright Office?
☐ **Yes** ☐ **No** If your answer is "Yes," why is another registration being sought? (Check appropriate box) ▼
a. ☐ This is the first published edition of a work previously registered in unpublished form.
b. ☐ This is the first application submitted by this author as copyright claimant.
c. ☐ This is a changed version of the work, as shown by space 6 on this application.
If your answer is "Yes," give: **Previous Registration Number** ▼   **Year of Registration** ▼

5

DERIVATIVE WORK OR COMPILATION Complete both space 6a and 6b for a derivative work; complete only 6b for a compilation.
a. Preexisting Material Identify any preexisting work or works that this work is based on or incorporates. ▼

b. Material Added to This Work Give a brief, general statement of the material that has been added to this work and in which copyright is claimed. ▼

See instructio
before compl
this space.

6

—space deleted—

7

REPRODUCTION FOR USE OF BLIND OR PHYSICALLY HANDICAPPED INDIVIDUALS A signature on this form at space 10 and a check in one of the boxes here in space 8 constitutes a non-exclusive grant of permission to the Library of Congress to reproduce and distribute solely for the blind and physically handicapped and under the conditions and limitations prescribed by the regulations of the Copyright Office: (1) copies of the work identified in space 1 of this application in Braille (or similar tactile symbols); or (2) phonorecords embodying a fixation of a reading of that work; or (3) both.

a ☐ Copies and Phonorecords   b ☐ Copies Only   c ☐ Phonorecords Only

See instructio

8

DEPOSIT ACCOUNT If the registration fee is to be charged to a Deposit Account established in the Copyright Office, give name and number of Account.
Name ▼   **Account Number** ▼

CORRESPONDENCE Give name and address to which correspondence about this application should be sent.   Name/Address/Apt/City/State/ZIP ▼

Area Code and Telephone Number ▶

Be sure to
give your
daytime ph
◀ number

9

CERTIFICATION* I, the undersigned, hereby certify that I am the
Check only one ▶
☐ author
☐ other copyright claimant
☐ owner of exclusive right(s)
☐ authorized agent of _____
Name of author or other copyright claimant, or owner of exclusive right(s) ▲

of the work identified in this application and that the statements made
by me in this application are correct to the best of my knowledge.

Typed or printed name and date ▼ If this application gives a date of publication in space 3, do not sign and submit it before that date.

date ▶ _____

☞ Handwritten signature (X) ▼

10

MAIL CERTIFI-CATE TO

Name ▼

Number/Street/Apartment Number ▼

City/State/ZIP ▼

Certificate will be mailed in window envelope

YOU MUST:
• Complete all necessary spaces
• Sign your application in space 10
SEND ALL 3 ELEMENTS
IN THE SAME PACKAGE:
1. Application form
2. Nonrefundable $20 filing fee
   in check or money order
   payable to Register of Copyrights
3. Deposit material
MAIL TO:
Register of Copyrights
Library of Congress
Washington, D.C. 20559-6000

The Copyright
has the authority
just fees at 5-yea
vals, based on ch
in the Consumer
Index. The next i
ment is due in
Please contac
Copyright Office
July 1995 to date
the actual fee sch

1

*17 U.S.C. § 506(e): Any person who knowingly makes a false representation of a material fact in the application for copyright registration provided for by section 409, or in any written statement filed in conne
with the application, shall be fined not more than $2,500.

July 1993—400,000   ♻ PRINTED ON RECYCLED PAPER   ☼U.S. GOVERNMENT PRINTING OFFICE: 1993-342-582/8

- **PA—Performing arts.** Form PA is for works such as plays, screenplays, multimedia works, song lyrics, and musical compositions.

- **SR—Sound recordings.** Form SR is for registering works such as musical and dramatic recordings.

- **SE—Serial publications.** This form is used for works such as newspapers, magazines, newsletters, and other periodicals.

- **VA—Visual art.** Form VA is for registering pictorial, graphic, and sculptural works.

What is the "best edition" of your work?

The best edition of your work is the highest-quality version of your work available at the time of registration. For example, a hard copy if also in paperback, a final draft of your manuscript rather than first draft, a compact disc rather than a cassette tape.

When can you send only one copy?

You must submit two copies of your work except in the following instances: your work is unpublished, is a multimedia work, was first published outside of the United States, is advertising materials, lectures, sermons, speeches, tests and test answers published separately from each other.

How must you pay your fee?

Send a check or money order in the amount of $20 made payable to Register of Copyrights with your deposit copies and completed form. If you have more than 12 transactions, you may establish a deposit account. Your fees will then be deducted at the time of transaction. To open a deposit account, obtain Circular R5 from the Copyright Office, complete the application form, and submit $250.

Testing electronic recordation

On February 27, 1996, a student at Carnegie Mellon University tested the Copyright Office Electronic Registration, Recordation & Deposit System (CORDS) for the first time when she transmitted a digital copy of her dissertation, plus an application for copyright registration for the work. She completed the form online and "signed" it using public key/private key encryption technology. The entire submission took only a matter of minutes, and a copyright registration certificate was expected to be returned within a few days, rather than several months under the manual application process.

"Once fully implemented, the CORDS system will aid both the Copyright Office and copyright owners by providing an efficient new registration and recordation mechanism," says Register of Copyrights, Marybeth Peters. For further information, contact the Copyright Office at 202-707-6737.

Notice of copyright

The notice of copyright—which generally includes the familiar encircled "c"—should always include the year of publication and the name of the copyright holder. It's like putting your name on the mailbox or hanging your shingle out. The copyright notice was once a requirement for copyright protection by law. However, in March 1989 the United States adopted the Berne Convention Treaty rule and eliminated the notice of copyright as a requirement for copyright protection.

Although the notice is not required, it is highly recommended. Consider it your "No Trespassing" sign for those who might be thinking of coming onto your property. While most people know they don't have a right to use your property, the sign sends a stronger message that you won't tolerate trespassing. Thus, the notice of copyright sends a message that you are well-aware of your rights and they'd better not mess with you!

What are the elements of a copyright notice? For a copyright notice to be valid, it must contain the following three elements:

♦ The symbol © (the letter C in a circle), the word "Copyright," or the abbreviation "Copr."

♦ The year in which the work was published.

♦ The name of the copyright owner.

Here are three examples of a copyright notice:

1. Copyright 1997 The Permissions Group.
2. © 1997 The Permissions Group.
3. Copr. 1997 The Permissions Group.

What is the public domain?

"The public domain is like a vast national park...without a guide for the lost traveler...or clearly defined roads," says M. William Krasilovsky in *The Business of Music*. There is a wealth of intellectual property free for the taking.

When the Statute of Anne broke the monopoly of the Stationers' Company's copyrights in 1709, one of the results was the creation of the public domain. Copyright was no longer in perpetuity. Once the term of copyright expired, the work was free for anyone to use. What types of creative works are not protected by copyright?

♦ Works with expired copyrights.

♦ Works consisting solely of facts or ideas.

♦ Works created by United States government officials or printed by the Government Printing Office.

Because these works are free for anyone to use in any way they choose, they can be a valuable commodity. Because the material can be adapted, it proves to be a good source for a great deal of newly copyrighted works. Consider how many film versions have been produced based on Louisa May Alcott's *Little Women* or Shakespeare's *Romeo and Juliet*. And how many cartoons and movies have been created by Disney from public domain fables and fairy tales such as "Beauty and the Beast" and "Aladdin."

When looking for public domain material to exploit and create your own copyrights, you need to be aware of a few things:

1. Know where you will be distributing your works

Understand the copyright laws present in other countries if distributing outside of the United States. Foreign law can be quite confusing, and works may have different copyright status in different countries.

For example, you may want to reprint "The Lake Isle of Innisfree" by W. B. Yeats in a novella you are writing. Although the poem was part of an 1893 collection of his work, it is in copyright in the United States. Permission to use the poem would come from the poet's publisher, Scribner. However, if you are distributing the work outside the United States, you will want to know that Yeats's works that were published during his lifetime are in the public domain in Canada. However, throughout the European Union his works are still in copyright until 2009. (Yeats died in 1939 and the protection in Europe is the life of the author plus 70 years.)

2. Be careful of translations and retellings

Works in the public domain that have been translated or retold may have a new copyright and require permission.

There may be many retellings of Aesop's Fables. It is not true that a fable is a fable is a fable. Check the copyright notice of these works and determine what is in copyright.

3. Be careful of introductory material, editorial notes, or changes

Whenever new material is added to a public domain work, that new material may well be in copyright. Any special editing or changes to the material may also be granted copyright protection. Examples: Robert Kimbrough's preface to the Norton Critical Edition of Joseph Conrad's *Heart of Darkness,* or the explanatory footnotes in the Riverside editions of Shakespeare's "Macbeth."

Out of the public domain?

Two recent changes in legislation throughout the world have made it even more difficult to determine the copyright status of works.

♦ In England, the term of copyright was extended from "life plus 50 years" to "life plus 70 years." Some works by authors such as James Joyce, Rudyard Kipling and A.E. Housman have regained copyright protection.

♦ On January 1, 1996, as a result of the General Agreement on Tariffs and Trade, commonly known as the GATT Treaty, certain foreign works that had lost copyright status in the United States, were brought out of the public domain. A list of those works can be found in the *Federal Register,* beginning May 1, 1996, and subsequently every four months thereafter. They can also be found on the U.S. Copyright Office Home Page at http://lcweb.loc.gov/copyright.

What is fair use?

If you had to get permission every time you wanted to use a few words from a book in a term paper...or needed to make a single copy of an article to read once you left the library...or sang a few bars of "Blowin' in the Wind" while you drove down Highway 61—life would be a drag. Because such a tight (and ridiculous) hold on intellectual property would stifle learning and creativity, the copyright law does have limits to the exclusive rights of a copyright holder.

Section 107 of Title 17 states that the fair use of a copyrighted work, including using copyrighted material for purposes such as criticism, comment, news reporting, teaching (including multiple copies for classroom use), scholarship, or research, is not a copyright infringement.

This does *not* mean that all educational, research or news reporting uses are fair. Section 107 states that at least four factors must be considered in determining whether a use is a fair use:

1. The *purpose and character* of the use, including whether such use is of a commercial nature or is for nonprofit or education purposes.

2. The *nature* of the work.

3. The *amount and substantiality* of the portion used in relation to the work as a whole.

4. The *effect of the use* upon the potential market for or value of the work.

The key to determining fair use is the word "fair." Would the author of a copyrighted work think that the way in which you intend to use his or her material is fair?

Consider the following situations:

♦ A fashion designer wants to use short phrases from works of Gertrude Stein on tags for a line of Zen clothing. The amount of the material is small, but the purpose and character of the use is for commercial gain. Would Gertrude Stein want her work to benefit a clothing manufacturer or designer?

♦ A writer wants to include some passages from private letters of John Lennon in an article she is writing for *Rolling Stone*. Although the passages are brief, the letters by *nature* are private. It would not seem fair to the estate of John Lennon to use the material without permission.

♦ It is often thought that anything under 250 words is fair use. What about 55 words? Did you know that 55 words represents one-half of Robert Frost's poem, "Stopping by Woods on a Snowy Evening?" This small *amount* of words is a *substantial* portion of Robert Frost's work.

♦ A professor wants his students to read "A Clean, Well-Lighted Place" by Ernest Hemingway. He asks the students to copy the story out of an anthology in the library. The professor may argue that the copying would be for educational purposes, but Hemingway's publisher, Charles Scribner's Sons, could certainly cite a loss of royalty income from the lost sales as an effect the copying had on their property.

Beware! Anytime you adapt copyrighted material without permission you are taking a risk. The copyright law and doctrine of fair use are written in broad language and open to interpretation. The only true determination of whether something is a fair use would be decided in a court of law. Give careful consideration before claiming fair use. When in doubt, don't!

International Law

This book discusses the United States copyright law and its ramifications for copyrighted works published or created in the United States. As the walls of our global village come down, it is even more apparent that we need to be familiar with international copyright law. With the click of a key stroke we can distribute copyrighted material around the world and, conversely, we can print copyrighted material from around the world.

There is no common copyright law in the world. Each country has its own laws. Through international treaties, countries have agreed to give each other the same copyright protection they give to their own country. The two major treaties are the Berne Convention for the Protection of Literary and Artistic Works and the Universal Copyright Convention. The United States has been a member of the UCC since September 16, 1955, and joined the Berne Convention on March 1, 1989.

If you are planning on distributing your copyrighted works outside of the United States, you will need to know the copyright law of the countries in which you will be distributing. One good resource for more information on the treaties and international law is *The Copyright Handbook Second Edition* by attorney Stephen Fishman. (See Appendix A.)

Moral rights

The copyright law in many European and other countries grants to authors additional rights. These rights are known as moral rights or *droits morals*. Moral rights are different from the economic rights granted in U.S. law in that they do not terminate and cannot be transferred, even if copyright has been transferred. They are the artist's rights in perpetuity and pass on to the heirs. What are these moral rights?

- The right to prevent modification, distortion, or mutilation of the work in a way that would harm the artist's reputation or honor.

- The right of the artist to insist that his or her name be affixed on the work or *not* placed on works that are not theirs.

- The right of the artist to determine all aspects of public presentation of the work.

- The right of the artist to withdraw or disavow any work if it is changed or no longer represents the artist's idea.

Summary

Whether you are creating original works that you want to protect or are using the copyrighted works of others, it's important to understand the basics of copyright law. Some of the key points we covered in Chapter 3:

There are two U.S. copyright laws you need to be familiar with: One governs works published before 1978; the other after 1978.

Highlights of the old law:

- Publication was the key to protection.

- A term of copyright was 28 years, with a 28-year renewal for a total term of 56 years.

- Works must have displayed a valid copyright notice to be protected.

- A copyright had to be registered to be protected.

Highlights of the new law:

- Creation in fixed form is the key to protection.

- A single term of copyright-life of the author plus 50 years for individuals, or 75 years from publication or 100 years from creation (whichever is first) for a company.

- Notice of copyright is optional after March 1, 1989 (although strongly recommended).

- Registration of copyright is optional (although strongly recommended).

- In 1992, copyright law was amended to include automatic renewal.

- Works are registered with the U.S. Copyright Office. If you have registration questions, you may call the office in Washington, D.C., at 202-707-3000.

- Electronic recordation is being tested. For more information about CORDS, call the Copyright Office at 202-707-6737.

- A notice of copyright is advisable to let others know who owns the copyright to a given work.

- Knowing what material is in the public domain can be tricky. When in doubt have a copyright search performed.

- Be aware of the four factors of fair use:

  1. The purpose and character of the use.
  2. The nature of the work copied (or used).
  3. The amount and substantiality taken.
  4. The effect of the use on the market for the original work.

- Fair use is sometimes an overused concept. Don't claim fair use lightly. When in doubt, request permission to use copyrighted material or consult a copyright professional.

4

Fair Use Examined

Perhaps the most frequently asked copyright question is: What is fair use? It seems as though most people understand that the property belongs to someone else, they just want to know how much they can use before they have broken the rules.

The four factors of fair use

A case of copyright infringement has been filed. The parties involved in the suit must bring their sides of the case to the court. The defense has claimed that the use of the copyrighted material was a fair use. The court will view the case through the paradigm of the four factors of fair use:

1. What is the *purpose and character* of the defendant's use?
2. How *much* of the plaintiff's material is used and how *substantial* is the use?
3. What is the *nature* of the use?
4. Does the use have an *effect on the existing or potential market* of the plaintiff's material?

Are tattoos a public display?

Never one to flee from controversy, Chicago Bulls basketball player Dennis Rodman took one of his protests to a different type of court. A federal court granted Rodman's request to stop a T-shirt company from marketing a shirt that featured replicas of Rodman's celebrated tattoos, which were arranged on the shirt just as he has them on his body.

In another tattoo twist, one of Dennis Rodman's fans came to a Bulls game sporting a tattoo of Rodman himself. The tattoo was based on a photograph of an outdoor billboard of Rodman and other Chicago celebrities, advertising the clothing chain Bigsby & Kruthers. During a radio interview, the tattoo artist who created the Rodman likeness exhibited his own lack of concern for copyright by stating that customers could bring in any photo to be re-created on the body part of their choice.

Tattoo art raises a number of copyright questions:

♦ Because human beings regenerate their skin periodically, is a tattoo really in fixed form?

♦ Do tattoos constitute a public display? What if they're covered by clothing?

♦ Because a tattoo creates a work in a new medium (body art), can it be considered a transformative work?

Let's consider the four factors of fair use: purpose and character; nature; amount and substantiality; and effect on the market for the original.

In the case of the Rodman tattoo taken from the clothing store ad, the purpose and character of the use by the fan was simply to show loyalty to Rodman and the Bulls, not for any commercial gain. The nature of the copyrighted work was an advertising billboard, not something intended for private viewing by a limited number of

---

(cont.)

people. You might make a case about the amount and sub-stantiality of the work, as the tattoo artist recreated the majority of the original. The effect of the use on the market or value of the original work (and Dennis Rodman is nothing if not an original work) is probably nothing.

As for the T-shirts, the purpose of the manufacturer was to make money using Rodman's likeness. And the existence of the shirt might affect the market for a similar shirt if Rodman decided to license one.

Let's take a look at a few scenarios in which fair use is a key player.

A word from President Gerald Ford

A common misconception is that it is the number of words you want to use that determines fair use. "It's only 300 words, so it must be fair use. It's such a small amount." When determining fair use, you must consider all four of the factors.

In 1985, the Supreme Court ruled that the use of even a small amount of words from a substantial work was *not* a fair use. *The Nation* magazine had used about 300 words from the 200,000-word memoirs of former President Gerald Ford (which was scheduled to be published by Harper & Row, Publishers, Inc.) in a story about Ford's decision to pardon former president Richard Nixon. Harper & Row sued *The Nation* for infringing its copyright. Although *The Nation* argued that it was merely reporting the news (a favored use under the Section 107 fair-use test), Harper & Row argued that the use of the material in the article had a significant effect on the market of its property.

Time magazine had contracted with Harper & Row for a fee of $25,000 to run the "Nixon pardon" material. After *The Nation* article ran, *Time* canceled its contract and refused to pay the balance owed of $12,500. In a 6-to-3 decision, the Supreme Court held that *The Nation* had indeed violated copyright and that a fair-use defense did not apply. Justice Sandra Day O'Connor stated that fair use applied in a much narrower way because the material was from an unpublished work, quoting even this small percentage of material violated the law.

Are databases copyright-protected?

A health care provider network has developed a database containing a variety of information including drug interaction information. Some of this data is published in the network's quarterly newsletter. Another network extracted this information from the newsletter and added it to its database of information. Is this use fair? Or is it infringing?

Prior to a landmark Supreme Court ruling, the "sweat-of-the-brow" determination in fact-gathering would probably have helped determine the outcome. On March 27, 1991, however, a U.S. Supreme Court decided unanimously that Feist Publications, a Kansas-based publisher of directories, did not infringe on the Rural Telephone Service when Feist copied the Telephone Service's white pages.

Justice Sandra Day O'Connor, writing for the court, said, "The only conceivable expression is the manner in which the compiler has selected and arranged the facts. Thus, if the selection and arrangement are original, these elements of the work are eligible for copyright protection. No matter how original this format, however, the facts themselves do not become original through association."

The key consideration when determining the copyright-ability of a database is original authorship—*how* the facts are selected and arranged. An alphabetical listing of all persons residing in a city, such as that published by Rural Telephone Service, does not exhibit any original authorship. Yet, if you select from that list all residents who subscribe to *The New Yorker* magazine and are over the age of 35 you may have added authorship to the database you have created.

What is a database?

An automated database is a body of facts, data, or other information assembled into an organized format suitable for use in a computer and comprising one or more files.

The copyright law does not specifically enumerate databases as copyright-protected, but the legislative history indicates that Congress considers computer databases and compilations of data as "literary works" subject to copyright protection. Databases may be considered copyrightable as a form of compilation, which is defined in the law as a work "formed by the collection and assembling of pre-existing materials or of data that are selected, coordinated, or arranged in such a way that the resulting work as a whole constitutes an original work of authorship."

Source: Circular 65, "Copyright Registration for Automated Databases," U.S. Copyright Office.

Parody and fair use

A parody, according to *Webster's New World Dictionary*, is a "literary or musical work imitating the characteristic style of some other work or of a writer or composer in a satirical or humorous way, most typically by applying it to an inappropriate subject."

From Tom Stoppard's spin on Shakespeare (*Rosencrantz and Guildenstern are Dead*), to Anthony Hecht turning Matthew Arnold's poem *Dover Beach* into the *Dover Bitch*, to Weird Al Yankovic's derivative work of Michael Jackson's *Beat It* into *Eat It* (let it be known that Weird Al does get permission to make his adaptations), parodies have provided social commentary, criticism, and entertainment throughout history.

Parodies can serve the function of keeping certain artists or works from seeming too important. For example, while *American Gothic* has remained Grant Wood's creation, it is difficult to view the painting and not think of the myriad of parodies that have been created based on the painting.

The legal loophole utilized by parodists is the doctrine of fair use. While parody is not directly mentioned in the Copyright Act, scholarship and commentary are both allowable exceptions to the law.

The guidelines used to identify whether a work can be seen as a parody and receive protection under the fair use provision of the Copyright Act include the following:

♦ The work may contain only enough of the original work to make it identifiable as a parody.

♦ The parody must create a new work that can stand on its own, while criticizing the original work.

What if the new work is in bad taste and its existence may hinder the sales of the original work? While a parody's effect on the market for the original work is weighed when cases are heard, the Supreme Court maintains that if a work is identified as a parody, it will have a different market than the original work and should not hinder sales.

Therefore, Anthony Hecht was within his rights when he turned Matthew Arnold's love interest in *Dover Beach* into a prostitute in his parody *Dover Bitch: A Criticism of Life*. As were the writers of *Saturday Night Live* when they parodied the song *I Love New York* called *I Love Sodom*.

Parody as an art form has come under a great deal of scrutiny in the last few years, largely as a result of *Campbell v. Acuff-Rose* or, as it is better known, the case of *Pretty Woman*. The rap group 2 Live Crew took its right to create a parody (their rendition of Roy Orbison's song *Oh, Pretty Woman*) all the way to the Supreme Court.

One of the central issues examined in the *Pretty Woman* case was the definition of a derivative work. After refusing the rap group permission to record the song, *Acuff-Rose* filed an infringement suit, claiming that the group's version of the song was an unauthorized derivative of the original work. The group claimed that its song was a parody and, therefore, it represented a fair use of copyrighted material.

After four years in various courts, the Supreme Court upheld an artist's right to parody original works under existing fair use doctrine. Justice David Souter referred to the work as "transformative." "Transformative" has become part of the fair-use test. It is different from a derivative work; the right to create derivative works belongs to the copyright owner. The more transformative the second work is, the more likely it will be considered fair use.

Although the Supreme Court upheld the right to comment or criticize original works through the creation of parodies, simply calling a work a parody does not guarantee protection against an infringement suit. The courts will continue to have the final say on whether a use is fair.

A word of caution: Fair use is about risk. How much risk are you willing to take? How much time and money are you willing to expend to defend your risk? Would it be worth the trouble? Wouldn't it be better to spend a few dollars for permission rather than countless dollars in court?

You've reviewed your use through the four factors. You are still not sure if your use is a fair use. If there is any doubt in your mind, it may be wise to paraphrase or request permission.

Summary

One of the most misunderstood (as well as overused) concepts in copyright law is that of fair use. Here are some of the keys to remember:

♦ Section 107 of the copyright law identifies four factors that must be considered when claiming a fair use of copyrighted material: the *purpose* and *character* of the use; the *amount* and *substantiality* of the use; the *nature* of the use; the *effect* of the use on the market for the original. Courts may also consider other factors in determining whether a use is fair.

♦ The Gerald Ford case proved that even a very small amount (300 words out of a manuscript of 200,000 words) may not be considered fair use.

♦ A collection of factual information alone is not copyrightable. However, if the collection of data has authorship, or originality, then it is protected by copyright.

♦ Parody (the criticism or satirization of another's work) is protected as freedom of speech. However, simply claiming a work is a parody does not automatically protect it against a copyright infringement suit.

♦ When you claim fair use, you take a risk. The wording of fair use language in the Copyright Act is vague and subject to interpretation by the courts!

5

The Printed Word

When Johann Gutenberg invented the printing press in 1456, little did he realize that he was setting more than type in motion. Look around—print is everywhere, from books to magazines, from food labels to footwear! Clearly, the definition of "the printed word" encompasses much more than Gutenberg's Bible and other books mass-produced from a printing press. And, in turn, the protection afforded by copyright law covers much more than books and magazines.

As we discussed earlier, under the current copyright laws in the United States, words are copyrighted as soon as they are put in "fixed form." In addition to the books, magazines, and newspapers you buy at the bookstore, this might include a letter to your aunt, a poem from your sweetheart, your first-grader's story on her pet turtle, your son's dissertation, your accounting firm's marketing brochure, or your prepared acceptance speech for your Nobel prize.

Again, it's the *expression* of the ideas that is copyrightable, not the idea or the fact itself. In other words, if you have an idea for a story, a play, a poem, or a screenplay, and you don't write it down in some way, no matter how much you have developed it in your head, it's not protected by copyright.

Book publishing

Copyright is a key issue for anyone involved in book publishing, but particularly the writer, the creator of the intellectual property. Why? *Revenue*. For each sold book, the writer receives payment. If the work is copied, sold, or used in some way without the knowledge or permission of the writer, he or she loses the opportunity to profit from the work.

The National Writers Union expresses its concern about the dangers of copyright infringement, by describing "the decline in the standard of living of most writers, as well as of other creators—a decline due in large part to the stagnation, or outright decline, in pay; the theft of our work by large media corporations which commercially exploit our work and pocket the profit; and the seizure of an ever broader spectrum of rights by publishers who pay the same or less money than was paid for print publication rights."

Trade books vs. textbooks

An important distinction needs to be made between "trade" books—those books published to be marketed to the general public usually through bookstores—and textbooks, those books published primarily to be used in an educational setting.

With many trade books, the copyright remains with the author. The publisher buys the publishing rights, which means that for a period of time, as specified in the author's contract, the publisher has the right to control how and when the work is published. This may include the right to grant reprint permission when another author wants to excerpt or adapt the material in another book. (Although it is not the norm, some authors reserve the right to review all requests to have their material reprinted.) And when a book goes out of print, the rights generally revert to the author.

In terms of copyright, textbooks are viewed differently. Most trade books are generated by the author's idea. Textbooks are generally initiated by a publisher. Acquisitions editors employed by publishers work with teachers and professors to determine what types of books are needed in classrooms. The editor then finds the appropriate author and contracts with the author to write the book. Copyright generally stays with the publisher.

Subsidiary rights

Even though the primary product in book publishing is the *book*, copyright protection isn't limited to the book itself. As discussed in Chapter 2, the print rights are often only the starting point for a literary property. If a book sells well, it may prove marketable in other forms. For example, a popular fiction book may become a movie, an audio tape, or even a play. A nonfiction book that sells well may become an audio tape, a computer program, a training video, or even a multimedia CD-ROM.

The rights to negotiate separately for audio, software, foreign translation, or other rights are generally described in an author's book contract. Author or agent and publisher clarify which parties have the right to negotiate the rights for future products based on the original book. And in rare cases, the subsidiary rights can even be sold before the book is written. A savvy author will understand what rights are negotiable and how the revenue will be divided.

Anthologies and collections

What about a book featuring the writings of several individuals? Does the publisher of an anthology or other collection of works hold the copyright? Typically, the publisher holds *no* rights to selections in an anthology.

For example, an anthology of English literature may contain works by a variety of authors, essayists, and poets. Some of the material may be in the public domain (such as works published in the 19th century) and some may be protected by copyright. Those copyright-protected works generally appear "by permission" of the copyright holder. Unless the publisher of an anthology happens to be the copyright holder for some of the selections in the anthology, it holds no rights for the selections.

Then what does the publisher hold the rights to? The publisher of an anthology does control some of what goes into an anthology:

♦ Compilation, or the way the works are selected and compiled in the anthology.

♦ Cover art and any art created to accompany the text.

♦ Foreword, preface, chapter introduction, and any other material newly created for the anthology.

Anthology publishers are often bombarded with requests to reprint material to which they hold no rights. Typically they respond to such requests by referring the requester to the copyright holder—the owner of the underlying work. Often, they will simply send a letter referencing the request, followed by a box checked next to the sentence, "Not our material."

If you wish to reprint or use some material that appears in an anthology, you can often find the source of the material on the copyright page of the anthology. Here, the publisher may list the copyright information regarding the reprinted material appearing in the book. If there is no information here, you might check the acknowledgment page. Often, the publisher or the editor of the compilation will acknowledge the contributors to the work. If this doesn't offer any clues, you may then be forced to rely on the publisher to provide you with the information.

Tables, charts, and graphs

Many books, particularly nonfiction works, include graphic components—tables of information, pie charts, and elaborate graphs—that others may want to reprint or use. Often, the publisher does not own the copyright for these components. They may have been reprinted from other sources or provided by experts. Often, the publisher acknowledges the source with a credit line, on the copyright page or, possibly, in the acknowledgments.

Letters

Where F. Scott Fitzgerald once wooed Zelda with pen and paper, today's young lovers bill and coo via the fax machine. Parents no longer need to check the mailbox for letters from their dorm-bound college students—they need only check their e-mail or even visit their child's home page on the World Wide Web.

Regardless of how often they write letters, most people do not think of their everyday correspondences as having great literary value. But they may be surprised to learn that copyright law has always protected personal letters as a form of intellectual property.

The general rule regarding personal correspondence is that the author of a letter retains the ownership of the copyright, the literary property, while the recipient of the letter acquires ownership of the physical property (the paper and ink.) The author has the exclusive right to permit or prevent the copying of the letter and its publication. The recipient has the right to destroy or preserve the letter, show it to others, deposit it in a library or transfer possession of the physical property. This rule applies whether the author is Bill Gates writing a letter to the editor of *Newsweek* in response to an article about Microsoft, or a neighbor writing a letter to his brother to offer advice on growing prize-winning tomatoes.

While the copyright remains with the author, the time at which a letter was written is important in determining how reprint permission should be handled. Letters written before January 1, 1978 (the date the current copyright law was enacted) are protected under common law. As is the case today, the copyright for a letter is held by the author. However, the factor determining who holds the copyright is publication. If the letter was never published (as is the case with most letters), the copyright stays in perpetuity with the author and heirs. However, if the letter was published, the author holds the copyright for a term of up to 75 years, after which the letter is in the public domain.

Publication is not a factor in determining the term of copyright for letters written *after* January 1, 1978. Under the current law, letters are protected by copyright from the moment they are fixed in a tangible means of expression, such as on paper, regardless of whether they are ever published. Existing copyright law sets the term of copyright on letters as the life of the author plus 50 years.

However, under a special provision of the copyright law, works of original authorship that were unpublished as of January 1, 1978 are protected by copyright until at least December 31, 2002 (if the work remains unpublished as of December 31, 2002, copyright will expire 50 years after the author's death, or if the author died before January 1, 1953, copyright expires on December 31, 2002). This means that if a person wishes to use an unpublished letter that was written prior to January 1, 1978, he or she must obtain permission from the author or heirs at least until the end of the term of protection in 2002, but possibly longer.

This is of particular importance to historians, biographers, and other scholars. Consider the following real-life example: An educational textbook publisher wanted to include a letter written by George Washington in a history textbook. The letter was part of the George Washington Papers in the Manuscript Division of the Library of Congress. The permissions manager wrote for permission to reprint the letter in the text. She was informed that they could neither grant nor deny permission. The writer of the letter, under common law, had the sole right to publish the property, and that right had descended to his heirs. Finding the heirs of George Washington could prove difficult. Without their permission, publishing the letter would definitely be taking a risk.

In this case, the publisher decided that the letter was important enough to the book that it was worth the risk. If the heirs came forward, the publisher was prepared to take responsibility for including the letter without permission.

Scholarly writings

"Publish or perish." It's a familiar philosophy in the academic community. In order to maintain your professional reputation, it is essential to write—either books or articles for professional journals. Otherwise, you won't be as strong a candidate for tenure, department chair, etc.

As experts in their respective fields, college and university professors represent the cutting edge of research and thought, and offer the basis for further research by students and others. It is through their writings that new theories get proposed, debated, proven, or debunked. Medical journals such as the *Journal of the American Medical Association* are often looked to by the medical community as well as the media for the latest information on the diagnosis and treatment of disease and illness.

A professor's work moves from a doctoral thesis to a scholarly book with a limited printing to a college textbook with a large audience. So, too, moves the value of the work from a pure academic work to a more commercial property. A professor may want to incorporate other copyrighted materials into his or her work. He or she will have to receive permission to use the other work or pay royalties if using the other work is not a fair use. While the professor may have been able to claim academic fair use in his or her thesis, the textbook sold to 30,000 students creates a different situation.

Newspapers

The focus of most newspapers is to report facts—and facts are not copyright-protected. The first newspaper that reports the story of an airplane crash, for example, does not own the copyright to the facts. Anyone may read the facts from the newspaper, then write his or her own story. He or she doesn't even have to cite the paper as the source of the facts. However, the way in which the facts are presented is protected by copyright.

In fact, many newspapers do well because of the way they describe the facts of a given situation. *The New York Times* and *The Wall Street Journal* are popular because they are considered sources of highly reliable and well-written information. But whether it is a major expose, a feature on fashions, a comic strip, or a weather report, these tangible forms of expression are copyrighted.

The copyright to these works may not be held by the newspaper in which they appear. Newspapers use a combination of staff, freelance, and syndicated writers, artists, and photographers. A close look at the material in question can give clues as to the copyright owner. Does the byline say staff writer? Associated Press? Or Copyright 1997 King Features?

Magazines

While most periodicals have staff writers who contribute to the publication, many articles are written by freelance writers (as are some newspaper articles.) When a freelance writer sells a piece to a magazine for publication, he or she is often selling the "First North American Serial Rights." This means that the magazine is purchasing the rights to publish the piece for the first time in North America. The author generally retains the copyright to the article.

The rights are also considered "nonexclusive," which means that the author/copyright holder is free to sell the right to publish the piece in other publications, or perhaps in a book he or she compiles. The rights holder is also able to grant permission to others who wish to publish, excerpt, or adapt the work in another publication, such as a textbook, anthology, or other collection. (Once again, know who holds the rights before you request reprint permission.)

Work for hire

Who owns the copyright to a contributed work? This can be confusing. Is it a work for hire? Or does the author own the rights? If the author is an employee of the company publishing the work—be it a magazine, feature, news story, corporate newsletter, or marketing brochure—and the work is done as part of the employee's duties on the job, the copyright belongs to the employer. However, if the author is not an employee of the company publishing the work—if he or she works as an independent contractor hired only for specific projects—the copyright issue may not be as clear. Consider the following examples:

Example 1: A woman is employed as a copywriter in the marketing department of a large corporation. Her job responsibilities include writing articles for the company newsletter that goes to all of its employees. She writes an article about the company's wellness program for the newsletter. The article is well-written and well-received throughout the company. The author decides that the piece would fit well in the corporate news section of the city's major newspaper. Can she submit the article to the newspaper for publication?

Most likely the *company* owns the copyright to the piece because it pays the woman's salary and she wrote the article as part of her job. The company may be thrilled to have such a positive article about its commitment to employee health published in the paper. But as copyright holder, the employer must give permission before the work can be published.

Example 2: Let's look at the same copywriter in a slightly different situation. She still works for the same corporation in the same capacity. However, she also does freelance writing on the side. Inspired by the research she did for the piece on her company's corporate wellness program, she decides to write an article on smoking-cessation programs. She researches and writes the article during evenings and weekends. She writes her article and submits it for publication to the same major newspaper. The piece is published and she is paid the standard fee for pieces similar in length to hers. She owns the copyright to the piece for this and future publications.

Example 3: Our copywriter has left her full-time job to pursue freelance writing as a career. She is hired by her former employer to write another piece for the same newsletter she used to work on. She negotiates the right to retain copyright on the piece. The company pays her slightly less for the piece, but she maintains ownership as well as the right to sell the piece again.

Electronic communication and freelancers

The growth of the Internet has added a new dimension to freelance writing, as well as a great deal of tension between freelance writers and the publications to whom they sell their work. For example, many newspapers have started online versions of their paper. They work with a particular service or they post their articles with an online database. The articles are then available for reading, printing, or downloading by online service members or Internet users, sometimes for a fee.

So what's the problem? Don't the freelance writers want their material distributed electronically? That's generally not the issue. The freelance writers sold only "First North American Rights" to the publication. The companies have allowed the work to be made available through the most easily accessible (and least-restricted) means of transmitting information in the history of the world. And the writers, the copyright holders, *aren't getting paid*. The writers contend that they never sold the electronic rights to their work, and that publishers are committing copyright infringement by posting their work without permission.

Protecting freelance writers

As the debate between writers and publishers continues, two organizations have joined forces to protect the interests of freelance writers. Early in 1996, the National Writers Union and the UnCover Company announced a partnership that will allow writers to receive royalties for articles ordered through the UnCover system.

UnCover represents one of the world's largest databases of magazine and journal articles, claiming 7 million citations from 17,000 periodicals. In order to handle the royalties generated by the new venture, the NWU created the Publication Rights Clearinghouse.

Tasini v. The New York Times

The rights of freelance writers have been tested in a landmark case between Jonathan Tasini, president of the National Writers Union and *The New York Times*. Tasini was named the plaintiff in a suit brought by members of the NWU against The New York Times Company, Newsday Inc., Time Inc., Lexis/Nexis, and University Microfilms Inc. The plaintiff filed suit against the defendants for copyright infringement.

At issue was the sale of works of NWU members, sold for First North American Serial rights and subsequently made available through online databases such as Lexis/Nexis, without the permission of the author—and without any compensation. The defendants claimed that by purchasing First North American Serial rights, they automatically had the rights to electronic republication rights.

As of press time, this case has not been decided.

This clearinghouse was formed primarily to support writers by helping them get paid for the use of their work. The UnCover system is the creation of the CARL Corporation, a for-profit organization developed out of the Colorado Alliance of Research Libraries. Both UnCover and CARL are wholly owned affiliates of Knight-Ridder Information, Inc.

In a March 1996 press release, Rebecca T. Lenzini, president of CARL Corporation, stated, "We have always been diligent about copyright fees. This exciting arrangement with the National Writers Union uses existing technology to make sure creators receive a fair share of the revenue from the emerging information industry. We are pleased to have the NWU as a partner in our mission of making journal and magazine material available both quickly and economically throughout the world, while affirming the principles of copyright."

NWU President Jonathan Tasini added, "We look forward to turning this model of copyright clearance into the standard of the electronic database industry. Publication Rights Clearinghouse also expects to share and develop collective-licensing solutions with other companies in the business of reusing the works of freelancers—whether via full-text databases, CD-ROMs or the World Wide Web."

UnCover is a searchable periodical database and delivery service. Articles can be delivered via fax in 24 hours or less. The UnCover Reveal Alert service is also available, which automatically sends the tables of contents from specific periodicals directly to a subscriber's e-mail box on a weekly basis.

Users search the database for free, but incur costs when articles are downloaded. The base rate (not including copyright fees) is $8.50 for articles ordered directly by users and $10 for articles ordered through the UnCover staff. Payment is made by major credit cards or through other billing or payment options. (See Appendix for contact information on the NWU and UnCover.)

Summary

The ability to copy and distribute the printed word has changed dramatically since the invention of the printing press. Words are now copyrighted as soon as they are "fixed." Regardless of what form of the printed word you are working with, here are some key ideas to keep in mind:

- The risk of infringement increases as the potential profit increases.

- Copyright holders must be diligent about protecting the rights to their words, because their words are their property, and property has value.

- Rights to the printed word don't end with publication or serial rights. A book may become an audio or video tape, a movie, a play, or even a CD-ROM.

- Don't assume that the copyright holder for a particular work is the same as the publisher of the book (or periodical) in which the work appears.

- Letters are protected by copyright, just as any other intellectual property.

- The key to the term of copyright of a letter is when it was written—before or after 1978.

- Freelance writers typically sell First North American Serial rights, which allows the periodical that purchases those rights to publish the work one time in their publication.

- Copyright ownership in contributed works can be confusing. Understand your written agreement clearly before signing.

- The marketplace for freelance magazine and newspaper articles is changing greatly with the advent of electronic delivery of information.

6

Visual Arts

Who owns the rights to Grant Wood's "American Gothic"? What rights are involved in creating reproductions or photographs of the painting? And who owns the rights to the newly created work? What about advertisements? Are they protected by copyright? Who owns the rights to family photos taken at a studio? They're of your family, so you should own the copyright on the photo, right? All of these issues fall within the realm of copyright protection of visual arts.

Defining works of visual art for copyright purposes can be a bit tricky. For example, some visual images are protected by copyright, but are not defined as a work of visual art. Copyright law defines visual art as:

◆ A still photographic image produced for exhibition purposes only, existing in a single copy that is signed by the author, or in a limited edition of 200 copies or fewer that are signed and consecutively numbered by the author.

♦ A painting, drawing, print, or sculpture, existing in a single copy, in a limited edition of 200 copies or fewer that are signed and consecutively numbered by the author, or, in the case of a sculpture, in multiple cast, carved, or fabricated sculptures of 200 or fewer that are consecutively numbered by the author and bear the signature of other identifying mark of the author.

A work of visual art does not include:

♦ Any poster, map, globe, chart, technical drawing, diagram, model, applied art, motion picture, or other audiovisual work, book, magazine, newspaper, periodical, data base, electronic information service, electronic publication, or similar publication.

♦ Any merchandising item or advertising, promotional, descriptive, covering, packaging material, or container.

♦ Any portion or part of any item described in the first two listings.

The Visual Artists Rights Act

For the first time, Congress accorded "moral rights" to creators of works of visual art with the Visual Artists Rights Act of 1990 (VARA). Although any original work committed to fixed form was already protected by copyright, VARA extended the rights of creators of visual art. Under VARA, the following acts are prohibited:

♦ Any intentional distortion, mutilation or other modification of the work that would be prejudicial to the artist's honor or reputation.

♦ Destruction of a work of recognized stature.

- ◆ Use of the artist's name with a work that the author did not create.

- ◆ Use of the artist's name with a work that has been modified.

VARA was enacted shortly after the United States joined the Berne Copyright Convention (see Chapter 3), which acknowledges an author's rights of attribution and integrity. These rights cannot be transferred, nor do they ever expire:

Say an artist is hired to paint a large mural for a community airport. Several years after the work is completed, the artist gains worldwide fame. The airport that commissioned the mural decides that the people who pass through the facility might want to purchase items depicting the mural painted by the now-famous artist, so it orders coffee mugs, T-shirts, and coasters bearing a replica of the mural and the name of the airport. Someone sends the artist one of the items bearing his artwork. Based on his rights under VARA, the artist has the right to stop the airport from producing commercial items using his art.

Before VARA, the mural would have been treated solely as a property. The artist would have had no say in this matter. Now, the author can even remove his name from the work. Moral rights, however, can be waived. The waiver should be in writing.

The scope of works covered under VARA is quite narrow, including paintings, drawings, prints, sculptures, and limited edition photographs. Works must be produced in a "limited edition" of 200 copies or fewer, with each piece being numbered and signed by the artist.

The following types of art are specifically excluded: posters, motion pictures, audiovisual works, books, magazines, databases, electronic media, advertisements, packaging materials, and any work that is not copyrightable.

Reproductions

If you created a painting or sculpture today (outside of a work-for-hire arrangement), you would hold the copyright to the work. But what about classic works, such as the "Mona Lisa" or "Blue Boy"? Those works are in the public domain. That means you can do whatever you want with them, right? Well, yes and no.

While it is true that the "Mona Lisa" is in the public domain, the actual painting is part of a collection housed at the Louvre in Paris. Along with the right to charge admission to view the works they house, the museum can control the rights to reproduce the works or to license those rights to others. This is why many museums won't allow you to take pictures of any or all the items in their collections.

If a work of fine art is protected by copyright, the copyright holder maintains (or can transfer) all the rights accorded to any copyright holder, including the right to reproduce and distribute the work. Therefore, before creating and marketing a necktie that features Dali's "The Persistence of Memory," find out who holds the copyright and ask for permission.

Photography

When Mathew Brady captured his famous Civil War images, little did he know what impact the medium would have on copyright and its issues. Whether it's a limited-edition Robert Mapplethorpe shot on display, an award-winning newspaper photo, or a family portrait taken in a studio, photographs are set in fixed form and are covered by copyright. Limited-edition photography (such as the Mapplethorpe print) are accorded additional protection under VARA.

Freelance/work-for-hire photography

Photographers generally hold the copyright on their work. If photos are taken while a photographer is working as an employee of a company, the copyright generally belongs to the employer.

Freelance photographers share many of the challenges of freelance writers (see Chapter 5). As with freelance writing assignments, concerns over who holds what rights can be avoided by the creation of a written agreement that outlines the rights of all parties at the outset of the job.

Many publishers go to great lengths (beyond the creation of a written agreement) to retain the copyright to photographs taken on their behalf, particularly with independent photographers. To fully establish their claim, some companies will provide photographic equipment and supplies and reimburse the photographer for mileage to and from the site.

Photography and the electronic age

With new technology comes new ways to commit infringement. Once an image is stored electronically, it can be easily downloaded, copied, and distributed. This can, of course, be a good thing for photographers, because it can make their work much more marketable.

But along with the benefits to the photographers come new issues. One involves photo archive services and long-term distribution agreements. Another concern is the way an image will be credited. When an image is stored electronically, the photo credit can easily be deleted. Perhaps the greatest concern is the increased ability to manipulate their images.

For more information on photo copyright, an excellent resource is *The Law (In Plain English) for Photographers* by Leonard D. DuBoff.

Studio photography

The effects of technology have even reached the local photo shop, many of which now feature "digital imaging" machines that allow users not only to duplicate any photo they bring in, but to alter the photo, including removing unwanted people. Now if a person gets divorced, but wants to preserve his or her own image in the wedding photos, he or she can go to the photo shop and have the ex-spouse cropped out! However—consumer beware—this may be copyright infringement.

"How can I commit copyright infringement with my own wedding photos? They're mine, right?" Consider the following scenario: You find a stack of photos showing family members from the World War I era. The photos are slightly cracked and faded, but you can still identify "Old Uncle Henry" and the tattooed lady the family legend says he dated. You've heard about a local photo shop that advertises a "digital imaging" machine that will not only reproduce the photos, but restore them to their original quality.

But you are told that the store will not reproduce the photos for you because the backs of the pictures are stamped with the name of the studio that took the photos. You must obtain reprint permission from the studio, which holds the copyright to the photos. You explain that the studio certainly went out of business many, many years ago. The photo shop manager suggests that you try to find the heirs of the studio owners.

While you are clearly not making a profit by cleaning up an old family photo (as opposed to scanning the photo for a book that will be sold to the public), the photo is protected by copyright because it is in fixed form. The exclusive rights of a copyright holder include the right to alter or reproduce the work. The right to alter the photo or make copies remains with the copyright holder—in this case, the studio.

Keep in mind that most camera store owners are not this familiar with copyright law. Many stores attempt to comply with the law by posting a notice on the wall and near the imaging machines themselves, describing the rights held by copyright holders. Yet the stores are put in a difficult position. They must comply with the law while not making the process so cumbersome that their customers will lose interest in the benefits of the new technology.

In a related case involving a copy shop, a freelance designer was preparing a brochure for an upcoming conference. He brought a photo of one of the conference speakers to the shop to have it scanned. The speaker himself had personally provided the photo. Unfortunately for the designer, the photo was stamped with the name of the studio that shot the photo. The copy shop would not reproduce the image without written permission from the studio.

Sculpture

A movie production company filming *Batman Forever* included some building shots in one scene. The film company got the required permits, including permission of the building owners at the locations of the shoots. And the right to film a building would include anything—including a sculpture—that happened to be on the property, right? Wrong.

The sculpture that caused the flap is titled *Zanja Madre* (meaning "Mother Ditch"), and was created by Minneapolis-based sculptor Andrew Leicester. The work appears in downtown Los Angeles, where part of *Batman Forever* was filmed.

Copyright law makes pieces of visual art, including sculpture, eligible for copyright protection. Warner Bros. was granted permission to film by the owner of the building in front of which the sculpture is located. However, the sculptor did not transfer his copyright to the building owner. Therefore, the right to film the sculpture was not necessarily included in the right to film the building.

Not only was the statue used in the film and the marketing materials, it was reproduced to scale for use in some of the film's scenes. Therefore, the use of the sculpture as part of the film was clearly intentional.

Cartoons and comic strips

Cartoons and comic strips have been a part of American life for almost as long as there have been newspapers. Characters like Blondie, Snoopy, Garfield and, more recently, Dilbert are as well-known as our sports figures or political leaders. Syndicated cartoons appear in newspapers worldwide and are reproduced in books regularly. Greatly enhancing the revenue picture is the licensing of products based on favorite characters from popular strips. But how are reprint rights for cartoons handled?

As authors and artists continue to fight for greater control over the copyright of their works, so are cartoonists engaged in an ongoing battle to hold on to what they create. The majority of major cartoon strips are controlled by syndicates, such as United Media (Peanuts, Garfield), King Features (Blondie, Beetle Bailey, Hagar the Horrible) and Universal Press (Doonesbury). It should also be noted that the major syndicates handle not only cartoonists, but syndicated columnists such as Mike Royko and Ann Landers. The copyright on most cartoons has been held by syndicates since William Randolph Hearst introduced the idea of syndication in the 1920s.

Syndicates have long been known for signing cartoonists to iron-clad, relatively one-sided contracts that leave artists with little or no control over their future work. Standard contracts give the syndicate all rights to the characters of a given strip, as well as the majority of the renewal options on the contract. In other words, a cartoonist who signs with a syndicate may no longer hold the rights to the characters he or she has created. If the artist is unhappy with the agreement, he or she is unable to take the strip elsewhere. If a cartoonist does leave a syndicate, the syndicate is often free to hire another artist to continue drawing the strip.

On the other hand, it would be a huge task for a struggling cartoonist to shop his or her work to the thousands of newspapers around the country. The syndicates do provide an invaluable amount of exposure to cartoonists, and handle the accounting for royalties and licensing agreements.

Most people would probably be surprised to know that the most successful cartoonist ever, Charles M. Schulz, doesn't own the rights to his famous Peanuts strip. However, years ago, Schulz successfully negotiated more control over his work than many other cartoonists have been able to, including a guarantee from United Media that the Peanuts strip will be put to rest after Schulz's death.

In recent years, a number of cartoonists have challenged the syndicates. The first came from Bill Keane, creator of Family Circus. Ever since he successfully regained the copyright to his work after threatening to file a very public lawsuit, other cartoonists have begun waging their own battles.

Cartoonists who have taken legal action against their syndicate include Cathy Guisewite of Cathy, Lynn Johnston of For Better or For Worse and Jim Unger of Herman. Unger won control of Herman and now operates his own firm, LaughingStock, which licenses reprints of Herman. Berke Breathed, creator of the popular strip Bloom County, won back control of his characters from the Washington Post Writers Group, then chose to retire the strip, assuring that the syndicate could not hire another cartoonist to draw his characters.

Licensing is a piece of the syndication picture that takes on great significance. With the decline in newspaper readership, some in the syndication business feel that the industry would not survive without licensing comic-strip characters for other merchandise. Revenues from merchandise such as Ninja Turtle lunch boxes, Garfield toys that hang from car windshields and Peanuts greeting cards, not to mention the rights to produce animated television shows and movies, can far outweigh the revenues that come from strip appearances in newspapers.

When requesting permission to reprint or use comic strips or characters from cartoons, the same rules apply as with other literary works. First, you must identify the copyright holder. The paper in which a comic appears is rarely the party that grants reprint permission. Most often, permission is granted by the syndicate that holds the rights. The name of the syndicate is generally printed between the frames of the strip, or somewhere along the border of a single frame cartoon. The next most important piece of information is the date the cartoon was printed in the paper. The date is generally drawn into the corner of one of the frames, along with the name of the artists who drew the strip.

Some syndicates are developing a cross-referencing system to identify the captions and subject matter of strips. This will be particularly helpful if the requester needs reproducible art, as most syndicates are unable to identify a specific comic without the date it was printed. So if you want permission to use a particular Peanuts cartoon, you can probably get permission from United Media. But until a cross-referencing database is in wide use among cartoon syndicates, you may have a hard time getting reproducible art for your publication if all you know is the dialogue that appeared in the cartoon and you don't know the date the strip appeared.

Painting and fine art

Before the Copyright Act of 1976, artists generally controlled reproduction rights to their original work, while a printer or other artist who copied the work controlled the rights to the copy or reproduction. This changed with the new law: Now, the artist (or the artist's heirs) retain the copyright for the original work as well as for copies or reproductions of the original work, unless the artist or heirs transfer those rights to someone else. In addition, all art works created after March 1, 1989 are protected by copyright, regardless of whether they have been registered with the Copyright Office.

Although the 1976 act helped to spell out artists rights, the application of copyright to visual art remains a complicated matter. Works published prior to March 1, 1989 that were not previously registered may have fallen into the public domain in the United States. However, those works may still be protected by copyright outside of the United States, where copyright laws vary greatly from country to country. In fact, some works that were previously in the public domain outside the United States may have come out of the public domain to regain copyright protection. There is clearly cause for confusion over pre-1989 works and whether reprint permission is needed for reproductions.

A significant change in copyright law took effect on January 1, 1996, as a result of the General Agreement on Tariffs and Trade, commonly known as the GATT Treaty. This new legislation brought certain foreign works out of the public domain in the United States and has restored copyright protection. (See Chapter 3 for more details on the GATT Treaty.)

Print advertisements

You're publishing a marketing textbook and you want to use some ads that have appeared in magazines and newspapers. No problem, right? Companies create ads in order to promote and sell their products. So, you're really doing them a favor by giving them more exposure. You probably won't even need permission, but you decide to ask just as a formality. Why would any company object to having their ad used in a textbook?

It's not hard to make such assumptions. After all, companies spend millions upon millions of dollars to advertise their products each year. So you might be tempted to assume that they would jump at the chance to have their ad viewed by thousands of students. And some companies *will* jump at the chance.

However, more times than not, corporations will have some very specific questions they want answered. Questions such as: "How is the ad being used?"; "Will it provide a negative example of anything?"; "Is it being used as an example of bad advertising?"; "What will the text say that surrounds our ad, and when can I see it?" And after they consider your request, some companies will refuse permission, for a variety of reasons. (As we will discuss in Chapter 11, copyright holders have the right to say no.)

Although advertisers are eager to promote their products, they want to market their product in a particular way, to a very specific segment of their market. Publishing an ad in your book might expose the product to an unwanted market segment. For example, a company that manufacturers alcoholic beverages may not want its products to be exposed to college students in a textbook. Another company might feel that you have interpreted its ad to convey a message that was not intended.

Another complication is the appearance of *people* in the ads. While some companies will grant permission for ads that don't feature people, the same company may not grant permission if models were used in creating the ad. In many cases, the company holds the rights to the ad itself, but the models who appeared in the ad have retained the rights to the use of their image. While model releases can be obtained, they can be accompanied by a hefty fee.

Some things to keep in mind when considering reprinting a company's ad:

♦ Most companies diligently protect the copyright on their ads, as well as their trademarks and the way they are used and displayed.

♦ Be prepared to do some legwork in order to identify the copyright holder for a particular ad.

♦ The permission process for ads can be tricky and lengthy. Start with a company's public relations or marketing department, although you'll most likely be referred to the legal department or the corporate attorney.

♦ If you are requesting reproducible art along with permission to reprint the ad, allow extra time, and anticipate having to work with the company's ad agency.

♦ Look for the most current ads possible. You're less likely to be refused if the company considers the ad to be in keeping with its current public image.

♦ Be prepared to have the company offer you an alternate ad that is more current than the one you requested.

♦ Request additional ads from a variety of companies, because you may get refused for some of the ads you request.

Summary

Understanding copyright protection for visual arts can be challenging. The rights for different types of visual art are often handled in different ways, and held by different parties. Moral rights are now an important consideration in the copyright of visual art. Here are some important things to keep in mind regarding copyright and visual art:

♦ The Visual Artists Rights Act (VARA) of 1990 spells out the copyright protection in relation to visual art.

   • A key component of VARA is that it protects "one-of-a-kind works" such as paintings, prints, photographs, drawings, and sculptures in single or limited editions of 200 or less.

   • VARA does not apply to a number of types of visual art, including promotional art, packaging, maps, posters, and technical drawings.

♦ Fair use, or the allowable use without having to ask permission, rarely applies to works of fine art.

♦ Regardless of how easy it may become to duplicate photographs, studios hold the rights to the photographs they have produced.

- Photo archives are a tremendous resource for finding a wide variety of reproducible images for use in your publication.

- When seeking permission for cartoons, identify the syndicate that holds the rights. And get the date the strip was published when at all possible.

- Companies are particular about the ways in which their print ads are used. Request the most current ads possible, and request alternates in preparation for refusals.

7

Performing Arts

The very word "performing" seems contrary to copyright. The law states that in order to be copyrighted, a work must be in "fixed form." In order for "performance" to fall within the protection of copyright, the motion of the performing needs to be fixed—stationary—to be protected. For example, it is not Baryshnikov's leap across the stage that is copyright-protected, but rather the frame of film capturing the leap that fixes the motion of dance. How are other forms of the performing arts copyrighted?

Motion pictures

Motion pictures are protected by copyright as an audiovisual work. Like the multimedia presentations described in Chapter 8, motion pictures pose complex and sometimes confusing questions regarding copyright protection.

Most major motion pictures involve a screenplay, the film itself, and a soundtrack. If the screenplay is based on another work—such as a novel, a play, or a short story (as many are)—those rights are probably held separately. In other words, the studio will have to receive permission from the author of the novel or short story to prepare a screenplay (a derivative work). Add choreography for a film with dance numbers and you have as many as five elements, each protected by copyright. And seldom will all of those rights be controlled by the same party.

In many cases, the screenplay may have been created in a work-for-hire situation, with the screenwriter hired to write the script based on a particular work or original idea. However, some screenwriters are able to negotiate to hold on to the rights to their work. The credits at the end of the film will often reveal who holds the rights. The credits will include, usually at the very end, the copyright notice of the film, which includes the name of the production company, which should hold some of the rights.

Screenplays

You have a great idea for a movie script. You spend six months of late nights formulating the plot (and crafting your Academy-Award speech). You send off your script and wait by the mailbox for the responses to pour in.

After a few months of disappointment you move on to other things and your hopes of fame and fortune are forgotten. Then you hear about a new movie that seems familiar to you, even though you haven't seen it. When you do, you realize that the story is strikingly familiar to that script you sent to a variety of production companies the year before.

It may just be coincidence. Or, maybe you are a victim of copyright infringement. And while it is true that putting your work on paper qualifies it for protection under the copyright law, your work must be registered with the Library of Congress before you can file an infringement suit. (As discussed in Chapter 3, just because you own the copyright to the work does not mean you can file suit. You can ask the infringing party to stop using your material, but you cannot bring suit unless the work is registered.)

Registration doesn't necessarily mean that no one else has written a similar story—or that you are entitled to damages if your material is used without your permission. But it does go a long way toward proving that you are the author of your material, as well as establishing when you created the material. (See Chapter 3 for more information on how to register your script with the Library of Congress.

An additional step that doesn't hurt in proving authorship is registration with the Writer's Guild of America. Members can register their scripts for $10; nonmembers for $20. For forms and instructions, call 202-707-9100 or 212-757-4360. Keep in mind, this is not a substitute for registration with the Library of Congress.

You can try to avoid problems from the start by including a letter with any scripts you submit. Include a statement that you are the copyright holder of the material submitted, and that you are submitting it for the consideration of the production company or studio for possible production. You can also state that you appreciate their consideration and that if you don't hear from them within a reasonable amount of time you will assume that the script did not meet their needs and will submit it to other people for consideration.

You will find sample letters, as well as more information about screenwriting, at the World Wide Web home page of SCREENWRIT: Screenwriting for Motion Pictures and Television. The Internet address is in Appendix A.

Theater

A local high school decides to put on the play, *A Young Lady of Property* by Horton Foote. One of the responsibilities of the play's producer is to get the appropriate performance rights to the play. Where does he or she start?

The script probably names the company handling the dramatic rights for the play, which may not be the same party that controls the publishing rights. For example, the publishing rights for *A Young Lady of Property* are controlled by Horton Foote's agent, the Barbara Hogenson Agency. However, the stock and amateur production rights are controlled by Dramatists Play Service, Inc.

The producer must request the rights in writing. The copyright holder will want to know the number of performances, anticipated number of attendees and the purchase price of tickets sold. Upon receiving the information and reviewing the request, Dramatists Play Service then will forward a contract with a fee quote based on the specifics of the planned performances. The fee quoted should include the performance rights, as well as rental or purchase of scripts, musical scores, and orchestration.

According to one producer of a community theater, rights fees make up approximately 20 percent of the budget for a given production. And while the cost of the rights is an important consideration, the overall balance of music in the production may weigh more heavily in the theater's decision to sign the contract.

When negotiating rights for productions, one must bear in mind that some contracts contain very specific stipulations regarding the performance of the work. For example, if a theater plans to put on a production of *Fiddler on the Roof*, it must use the specified choreography in the contract for the production.

Another factor that may concern the theater company is the stipulation that rights for a production can be pulled (as close as 30 days to opening night) if a larger production of the play or musical is coming to the area. Although this doesn't happen often, one Chicago area high school was forced to cancel its production of *Joseph and the Amazing Technicolor Dreamcoat* when the musical announced a return engagement to Chicago.

Dance and choreography

Although choreographers frequently copyright their works, only one major case has tested the law as it relates to dance. In 1986, Barbara Horgan, operating on behalf of the estate of George Balanchine, brought suit against Macmillan, Inc., which was planning to publish a book containing photographs of Balanchine's ballet, *The Nutcracker.*

Although choreographic work is not specifically defined in the Copyright Act of 1976, in the case of *Horgan v. Macmillan,* choreography was defined as "the flow of steps" in a dance. This case involved whether photographs of dancers in *The Nutcracker* infringed George Balanchine's copyrighted choreography. The court cited the Copyright Office, which stated that choreography represents a related series of dance movements and patterns organized into a coherent whole. If a dance is performed, it is not fixed. The steps are danced, then the moment is passed leaving only the memories in the minds of those who witnessed the performance. Consequently, the choreography must be written down (as a script or score), or the performance must be captured on film or in still photos that identify the uniqueness of the steps.

Videotapes

Suppose a father buys a copy of a Disney movie for his child at a local video store. Most people are aware that it is illegal to copy the tape for a friend. But as long as the father doesn't copy the tape, he can, as the owner of the tape, use it in any way he wishes, right?

This issue surfaced in a battle between day-care centers and the Los Angeles-based Motion Picture Licensing Corporation. The MPLC notified some 50,000 day-care centers that they must pay a licensing fee (approximately $300 annually) in order to legally show commercial videos as part of their curriculum. Childcare providers and angry parents objected to the licensing fees, arguing that either the center or the parents purchased the videotapes and, therefore, had the right to show them at the center.

Many people apparently agreed. *The Chicago Sun-Times* conducted a poll that indicated 89 percent of those responding felt that day-care centers should not be forced to pay a video licensing fee.

However unpopular such a licensing requirement may be, the right to control public performance of a work is one of the exclusive rights granted to copyright holders. In fact, most prerecorded videos include a licensing agreement printed directly onto the tape: "Warning! Licensed for private home exhibition only. Any public performance, copying, or other use is strictly prohibited."

After this controversy, a U.S. senator from California considered introducing legislation to exempt childcare centers from paying the licensing fees. However, this proved unnecessary when the Motion Picture Association of America (on whose behalf the MPLC was operating), announced that childcare facilities with 100 or fewer children would be granted a token license for public performance for $1 per year. (The original licensing requirement remains in effect for centers with more than 100 children).

Speeches

A single speech can provide a variety of copyright issues. For example, a person writes a speech. He or she types it out in order to deliver it as written. Clearly, the written speech is copyrighted as soon as it is fixed form. But what about the delivery of the speech? Once the speech is delivered to its intended audience, it's over. It wasn't in fixed form, so the delivery of the speech can't be copyrighted. However, if the speech is captured on audiotape, then the audiotape is copyright-protected. And if the speech was captured on film or video, that version of the speech is also copyright-protected.

But who holds the copyright on these various forms of the speech? The author of the speech owns the copyright on the words. Doesn't he or she also hold the copyright to the tape and the video? Not necessarily. If the speech was given to the general public and there were no restrictions on taping the speech, then the person who did the taping, whether audio, video, or both, probably holds the copyright to the version he or she taped. However, the person giving the speech may have something to say about it, as did the Reverend Jesse Jackson.

A featured speaker at the 1984 Democratic National Convention, Jackson delivered a speech that was recorded on videotape by Chicago-based MPI Home Video. MPI then marketed the tape, which it had titled, *Jesse Jackson: We Can Dream Again*.

Jackson filed suit against MPI, claiming it had violated his copyright. While Jackson's speech was surely in fixed form (even though he is an eloquent extemporaneous speaker), MPI's claim was that the speech was a "news event" and, therefore, not subject to copyright. After testifying in court, Jackson told reporters, "If anyone has the right to exploit the Jackson family for economic gain, it ought to be the Jackson family." The parties eventually reached an out-of-court settlement after MPI was prohibited from continuing to sell the video. Harvard Law School professor Arthur Miller, in an article in *The Los Angeles Times* (August 31, 1988), said that what would likely have been debated in the case was a conflict between Jackson's property rights in his speech and whether he gave up the rights by giving the speech in a public forum—national TV.

Summary

While performing arts seem to present something of a contradiction when it comes to copyright (how can a performance be in "fixed form"?), certain aspects of performances are protected by copyright. Here are some important points when considering copyright and the performing arts:

♦ A performance needs to be "fixed" in some form (video, audio, film, etc.) in order to ensure copyright protection.

♦ Motion pictures are protected as audiovisual works. However, the rights can be very complex and are held by different parties. Use the film's credits (when available) as a starting point to identify who holds which rights.

♦ The rights to perform a work are often held separately from the print rights for the same work.

♦ Most videotapes are licensed for private home use only. Any public performance without permission may be infringement.

♦ Speeches may be copyrightable if they are in fixed form (on paper, disk, video, audiotape, etc.). An extemporaneous speech that is not fixed in any way is not protected by copyright.

8

Music

Most people know that making copies of a favorite CD for each of their friends would constitute copyright infringement. But what about making just one cassette copy, to play in the car? What about restaurants that have piped-in music or nightclubs that feature a DJ? And how come they never sing "Happy Birthday to You" any more in a restaurant?

Personal use

You just broke down and bought that CD collection of Beethoven's Symphonies. Now that you have it, you also want to listen to it in your car, which doesn't have a CD player—only a cassette deck. And you'd also like to listen to it when you go running, but your portable stereo is also a cassette player.

One of the primary concerns of record companies and musical artists is, of course, revenues. If you begin making copies of a favorite CD, you may want to make more.

When you begin making copies for family members and friends, they no longer have any reason to buy the CD, and you have indeed had an effect on the sales of the work.

The Audio Home Recording Act

But thanks to the Audio Home Recording Act, which was passed by Congress in 1992, consumers can now legally make copies of sound recordings for their own personal use. The Act requires a built-in fee to be added to all blank digital tapes (3 percent) and to all digital recording devices (2 percent). The fees are collected and distributed to copyright holders, including record companies, publishers, performers, and songwriters.

Included in the act was the requirement of the inclusion of a Serial Copy Management System (SCMS) circuit to be included in all digital recorders. The circuit allows users to make copies of copyrighted works, but not to make second generation copies (copies of copies).

Musical scores and lyrics

There are many aspects to consider when exploring copyright and music. It's important to remember that music is often made up of several components. Lyrics are protected by copyright and are generally considered the same as a literary work, separate from the musical notation, which is also protected by copyright.

Add a new arrangement (the instruments you think will work best, a new tempo, etc.), and you've added another aspect of the song that is protected by copyright. On top of all that, the specific recording of a piece of music may be protected by its own copyright (as we'll discuss in more detail in the following section), apart from the other components.

The Rise and Fall of DAT Machines

As the saying goes, "Build a better mousetrap and the world will beat a path to your door." That is, so long as the Recording Industry Association of America (RIAA) doesn't get in your way.

Around 1986, the word began to spread about a new type of cassette deck that could make digital or "perfect" copies of recordings. The new machine could duplicate a compact disc without picking up any of the background noise that accompanies playback from standard cassette recorders. And not only did the tapes sound better, but they were smaller than standard audio cassettes and they could even record up to two hours of music. Sounds like the "better mousetrap" was born, right?

Although many consumers, as well as observers of the audio industry thought so, the RIAA did not. An all-out war was launched against the manufacture and sale of DAT machines in the United States.

One record company tried to introduce technology (and tried to get legislation passed to require the use of it), that would in effect "copy-guard" CDs so that they couldn't be copied. The guard involved the inclusion of a sound on all prerecorded music that was inaudible to listeners (supposedly), but that would cause a DAT to stop recording when the noise was detected. Sort of like the copy-guard on videos, which generally cannot be seen when viewing the tape but creates lines across the screen when the tape is copied. (The legislation didn't pass, in part because the technology didn't work.)

DATs eventually became available in the United States in the early 1990s, but the recording industry held off their introduction to the market long enough, as well as severely limited the number of pre-recorded DATs released, so that by the time the machines were available, most consumers had lost interest. While DATs are still available, their sales have never come close to what was originally anticipated.

What makes this trickier is the fact that some aspects of a piece of music may be protected by copyright, while other parts are in the public domain.

For example, "In My Time of Dying" is a traditional folk song that has been recorded by many artists, including Bob Dylan and Led Zeppelin. Dylan's version is a traditional folk rendition of the song. He does not list a writer for the song on the album label. In the liner notes, the song is referred to as a "traditional" song.

However, Led Zeppelin's version lists the four band members as the songwriters. Are the members of Led Zeppelin taking credit for material that is not theirs? This rendition is a major departure from the traditional song. The acoustic guitar has been replaced by electric guitars and a variety of other instruments have been added. The words are basically the same as the traditional song, and the basic melody is present in parts of the song. But musically, a new song has been created. Because the traditional song and its melody are probably not protected by copyright, Led Zeppelin is within its rights to use them as the basis for a new work, as it is within its right to claim copyright for the work.

In another example, a book publisher wants to publish a book of hymns. While the words to thousands of hymns are in the public domain, many are accompanied by music covered by copyright. If the publisher wants to avoid paying fees for each hymn for which the musical notation is covered by copyright, it has two basic options.

First, the publisher can search and find hymns that are accompanied by music not covered by copyright. Or, if the publisher believes a greater market exists for hymns with a more contemporary musical feel, it can use the traditional lyrics and hire someone to write new music to accompany them. Should the publisher decide to produce a CD to go along with the book, it can hire performers to record the hymns. The publisher would then hold the copyright to the book of hymns, the music commissioned, and the recording of the hymns.

Sound recordings

Even though a piece of music and its lyrics may be in the public domain, a specific recording of the music may be protected by copyright.

For example, all of the works of Johann Sebastian Bach are in the public domain. That includes musical notation, arrangements, and lyrics. The Chicago Symphony can perform a series of Bach's cantatas and not have to pay any fees. It can even record the performance and release a CD without paying anyone anything.

Of course, the Symphony wouldn't hold the copyright to the music, the lyrics, or the arrangement. However, it would hold the rights to its recording of the Bach pieces. Therefore, if anyone wanted to use a part of the Chicago Symphony's recording (for example, on a CD-ROM about the life and music of Bach), they would have to get a master recording license from the holder of the recording rights of that specific recording.

In one real-life example, a corporation wanted to use 10 seconds of Vivaldi's *The Four Seasons* in a multimedia sales presentation. Vivaldi's music is in the public domain, so there was no copyright issue there. However, the version the company wished to use was recorded by the Boston Symphony Orchestra.

When the company requested permission, it found that the orchestra required payment not only to use the piece, but to compensate each performer, plus double the performers' fee for the conductor. Determining the cost was well beyond the budget, the company purchased the license to use a stock recording of the same music—for a lot less money.

Compulsory Mechanical License

How does an artist obtain the rights to record a particular song? What fees does he or she pay? What if the copyright holder doesn't want a group to record the song, for example, because of artistic differences?

Section 115 of the Copyright Act contains a provision for licensing nondramatic musical compositions, called Compulsory Mechanical License. (The term "mechanical" refers to the mechanical reproduction of the sound.) This provision *requires* the copyright holder of a composition to allow another artist to record the song if all of the following criteria are met:

♦ The song is a nondramatic musical work.

♦ The song has been previously recorded.

♦ The previous recording has been released to the public as a phonorecord (meaning audio only).

♦ The use of the new recording will be in phonorecords only (phonorecords include tapes and CDs, according to the definition in Section 101 of the Copyright Act.)

The fee paid to the copyright holder is the statutory rate (determined by the Copyright Statute—the rules and regulations set forth by the Copyright Office). The rate has changed over the years. For example, from 1909 to 1976 the rate was held at 2 cents. The 1976 Copyright Act raised the rate to 2.75 cents and made further provisions for adjustment to the rate by the Copyright Royalty Tribunal, a committee that meets periodically to review the rate. The current rate is 6.95 cents—or 1.3 cents per minute of playing time or fraction thereof, whichever amount is larger.

However, while the law makes the provision for the recording of others' material, most copyright holders prefer to sign direct licenses with those wishing to record their songs. According to Donald Passman in his book *All You Need to Know About the Music Business*, "The compulsory license is almost never used. Record companies hate to use it because the monthly accounting provisions are too burdensome. The copyright holders (publishers) would rather give a direct license because they can keep track of it easier."

Royalty arrangements

A royalty arrangement is essentially a risk-sharing arrangement between a music publisher and an artist or songwriter. A piece of music is like any intellectual property in that it can be bought and sold. The copyright is generally held by the author/composer of a given piece. However, as with written works published by a book or magazine publisher, the recording rights to a composition are generally held by the artists' record company.

ASCAP, BMI, and SESAC

Songwriters make money from royalties, plain and simple. A songwriter's ability to make a living depends on his or her ability to collect royalties when the music is played. But how can an artist keep track of every time his or her music is played? Nightclubs, restaurants, bars, and other venues play music night after night. Do they keep track of the songs they play and send a check to each artist? Does an artist get thousands of small checks for each time the work is played in public?

Fortunately for all parties involved, there are licensing organizations that handle royalties for songwriters: ASCAP (The American Society of Composers, Authors and Publishers), BMI (Broadcast Music Incorporated) and SESAC (Society of European Stage Authors and Composers). The primary function of these organizations is to collect royalties on behalf of their members.

Each organization holds a specific type of performance rights, known as "small rights" (for performance in public places, as opposed to rights to put on a musical production using copyrighted songs). All establishments that wish to play copyrighted music in their place of business must purchase a license from the appropriate organization. The license allows them the right to legally play music from the catalog of the organization from which they purchased the license.

Here's how licensing fees translate into money in the pocket of an author or composer: Various organizations, including restaurants, night clubs, roller rinks, even funeral homes need to play copyrighted music as part of doing business. It would be far too cumbersome to pay each copyright holder each time a copyrighted song is played. Therefore, these organizations purchase a license that allows them to play any of the songs in the licensor's catalog.

♦ The licensing organizations collect royalties on behalf of their members who have registered their works with them.

♦ The licensors use a variety of survey methods to determine which works are played and how often.

♦ ASCAP, BMI, and SESAC then distribute the fees to their members.

♦ The licensors employ auditors to conduct on-site visits to determine when and where copyrighted music is being played, and if nonlicensed organizations are committing acts of infringement.

Recorded music is not the only form of music subject to license. You may realize that you seldom hear "Happy Birthday to You" sung by restaurant employees on patrons' birthdays. The reason is that the song is protected by copyright and singing it in a business establishment requires a fee.

In 1996, the leaders of ASCAP found themselves in the middle of a controversy after a letter was sent to some 6,000 children's camps. The purpose of the letter was to notify the camps of licensing fees required to perform any of more than four million songs that are protected by copyright, including such standards as "God Bless America," or even "Happy Birthday to You."

A number of the camps that received letters are not-for-profit organizations, including those affiliated with the Girl Scouts of America. ASCAP never intended to impose the licensing fees on not-for-profits. The intended target was large, for-profit camps, some of which operate like luxury resorts, according to Vincent Candilora, ASCAP vice president and director of licensing.

A major part of ASCAP's mission is to collect royalties from those who perform (or play) their members' music, then pass the royalties back to the songwriters and composers. While sometimes characterized as the bad guy for "limiting access" to popular music, ASCAP President (and three-time Oscar-winning songwriter) Marilyn Bergman states, "It has always been in the interest of our members to encourage the use of music everywhere—particularly by young people." ASCAP has stated that it was never its intention to bring suit against the Girl Scouts, nor to "license Girl Scouts singing around a campfire."

Irving Berlin, one of the founders of ASCAP, made it very clear how much he supported the work of the Girl Scouts and Boy Scouts of America, when he donated, in perpetuity, all his royalties from his song "God Bless America" to them. According to ASCAP, the royalties now total "many millions of dollars." "In the spirit of Mr. Berlin, we are seeking to meet with the leadership of the Girl

Scouts to rectify the misunderstanding which led to this unfortunate situation," says Bergman.

The director of one chain of camps made his feelings about ASCAP clear when he told his camp directors that they would either pay the licensing fees or start writing their own songs. The director stated that he believed the camps were in the business of building upstanding citizens, and that teaching them to respect the law was a good place to start.

Finding the holders of other rights

While ASCAP, BMI, and SESAC license primarily for "small rights," other groups, often music publishers, grant for mechanical and other rights. And although these organizations don't grant for these rights, they generally know who holds the rights for a given song by a given performer. This makes both organizations an excellent resource if you need to get permission for a piece of music.

Each of these licensing organizations has World Wide Web sites and searchable databases. ASCAP's "ACE on the Web" is particularly user-friendly. ACE is a searchable database of the songs licensed by ASCAP in the United States. For each song, ACE can usually provide you with the artists who have performed it, the other copyright holders, as well as names, addresses and phone numbers.

Summary

While most people are aware that copying and distributing tapes of pre-recorded musical works constitute copyright infringement, they may not be sure exactly what they can do with the music they purchase. Here are some important keys to remember when considering copyright and music:

♦ It's generally acceptable to make one copy of copyrighted music, provided it is for your own personal use and not for distribution to others.

♦ The Audio Home Recording Act allows for the digital copying of copyrighted music. Fees are built in to the sales of all blank digital media and digital recorders, which are collected and distributed to copyright holders.

♦ When considering the rights to musical scores and lyrics, keep in mind that some parts of a piece of music (for example, the melody) may be in the public domain, while other parts (the lyrics) may be protected by copyright.

♦ The rights to a specific sound recording may be held by different parties than those that hold the rights to the music, lyrics, arrangement, etc.

♦ Musical artists can record a "cover version" of any song through a Compulsory Mechanical License (section 115 of the Copyright Act).

♦ ASCAP, BMI, and SESAC are licensing organizations that collect royalties through licensing fees, which are then distributed to the organizations' members (musical artists, song writers, composers, etc.).

♦ ASCAP, BMI, and SESAC are excellent resources for identifying the copyright holder for a particular piece of music, or of a particular recording of a piece of music. These organizations have World Wide Web sites that make it easy to find the rights holders for the music you want to use.

9

Copyright in the Electronic Age

According to the *World Almanac* statistics for 1996, 37 percent of all U.S. households had personal computers. It also indicated that there were 30 million computers connected to the Internet, with more than eight million of those users accessing the World Wide Web. Dataquest Inc. of San Jose, California, estimates that nearly 70 percent of all homes with incomes over $100,000 are computer-equipped. The Software Publishers Association, whose members include most major software manufacturers, projects that more than 40 percent of all homes will be computer-equipped by the turn of the century.

It has been said that the average American processes more information in a single day than a person in the 17th century processed in a lifetime. Computers are a factor in virtually every aspect of human life, from grocery shopping to visiting the doctor, from choosing a family pet to communicating with your dorm-bound college student.

The computer boom has created a wide variety of spin-off industries and thousands of new companies. The way people work, play, shop, and communicate has been profoundly changed by the electronic age.

One element of American society that has not significantly changed with the advent of new technologies is copyright law. Although it has undergone four revisions, the copyright law created by our founding fathers to protect intellectual property is still in place and continues to provide the template through which all electronics-related copyright cases are viewed.

Can copyright law keep up with evolving technologies? While this issue is explored in more detail in Chapter 13, it is pivotal to a discussion of electronic rights.

Many people believe that copyright law is "technology neutral." They believe that software, Web sites, video games and CD-ROMs should be seen as intellectual properties, as are books, music, and other pre-electronic forms of recordation. If so, they are adequately addressed and protected under current copyright law.

Others feel that the law is woefully inadequate—that it is far too limited to address the issues created by an industry that breaks new ground and creates its own copyright issues every day.

In September 1995, a report was issued by the White House Information Infrastructure Task Force (chaired by then Secretary of Commerce Ron Brown), titled, "Intellectual Property and the National Information Infrastructure," commonly known as the "White Paper." The primary goal of the task force was to determine what, if any, changes needed to be made in existing copyright law in order to protect intellectual property in the ever-changing electronic age.

The task force gathered information from a variety of individuals and organizations, including representatives from academia, libraries, the legal community, individual creators, and copyright holders, and the publishing, broadcasting, entertainment, electronics, and telecommunications industries.

Although the task force recommended several amendments to the Copyright Act, it found the act "fundamentally adequate and effective." However, the debates over changing copyright law continue.

Software

As one of the fastest-growing industries in history, the computer software industry has created its own set of copyright issues. Software must be easy to use and easy for users to protect from damage (by making backup copies). Because most programs can be copied to other disks, the temptation to give copies to others or sell copies can be great. Unlike most other media, computer software can be recreated perfectly.

The ease of copying extends the temptation beyond making disks to loading programs onto more than one computer. This is not only infringing but probably breaches the license agreement that limits use to only one computer. Therefore, the temptation can be great for a business to buy one copy of a word-processing or database program, then copy it onto five, 10, or more computers in order to save the cost of buying multiple copies of the software.

However, as tempting as this practice may be, it constitutes a major act of copyright infringement and software piracy unless the company acquired a network license. The SPA estimates that software manufacturers have lost as much as $8.1 billion in a single year to piracy of business applications alone—a figure made even more staggering by the fact that total revenues for business application software in the same year (1994) was $8 billion. In other words, the manufacturers collectively lost more to piracy than they made in total sales.

Site licensing

One method of licensing that is often employed by schools and businesses is that of *site licensing*. For example, a school provides access to a word-processing program as part of its computer curriculum. A copy of the program is loaded onto each computer in the school's computer lab. A site license has allowed the school to purchase the rights to unlimited use of the product within the classroom or department. The school purchases a single master copy of the program, as well as accompanying documentation, then makes copies for individual users, copies the master directly onto each hard drive, or makes the software available through a network server.

A site license fee for a large organization can be costly, but should ultimately be less than the cost of purchasing individual software packages for each computer.

The details of each site license agreement can vary. Some agreements may involve a single payment, while others may require an annual renewal fee. A license agreement may or may not include software upgrades. An agreement may involve a flat fee for an initial number of copies, with an additional charge for each additional copy.

Like product upgrades, manuals are not automatically included in the negotiated agreement. An organization may constitute the "site" in one agreement, while a single department may be defined as the "site" in another. One particular licensing arrangement may require individual users to agree to terms and conditions of use, and another could involve a simple group purchasing discount.

To find out more about arranging a site license for an educational institution or other organization, contact your software dealer (although not all retailers are authorized to negotiate site licenses), or go directly to the software manufacturer.

The Software Publishers Association

The Software Publishers Association (SPA) has represented a large portion of the software industry for 12 years. SPA's membership of 1,200 companies and individuals is made up of software manufacturers and developers, as well as distributors, consultants, and other companies and professionals who provide services to the computer industry. The SPA provides networking opportunities via conferences and educational seminars, conducts market research, and offers special-interest groups. In addition, the SPA represents member concerns through lobbying efforts in Washington.

The SPA has launched the Internet Anti-Piracy Campaign (IAPC). "The IAPC maintains the SPA's traditional balance between education and enforcement. We first make contact in an effort to amicably resolve the matter, and only when absolutely necessary do we turn to litigation," said SPA President Ken Wasch. Details on the campaign, including the "Seven Warning Signs of Piracy" for ISPs, can be accessed via the SPA's World Wide Web site (http://www.spa.org, or call 202-452-1600).

A part of the cooperative arrangement between the SPA and the Internet providers it works with is the ISP Code of Conduct. According to the SPA, "This simple agreement asks that ISPs protect themselves from liability by stopping pirate activity on their systems. In return, SPA will attempt to contact the ISP if it receives a piracy report concerning it—before initiating other action."

In addition to working with Internet providers, the SPA offers educational opportunities to businesses (as well as home computer users) that wish to comply fully with copyright law. Stressing the cost-effectiveness of staying within the law ("Learn how to save your organization more than $100,000 in one day!"), the SPA offers the Certified

Software Manager course and certification. The day-long course is designed to make managers familiar with the basics of software licensing agreements, as well as the dangers of violating them.

The SPA provides a cooperative audit program. Companies make arrangements with the SPA to conduct an audit of the computers and software programs in order to identify potential licensing violations. The companies then have the opportunity to make voluntary changes or upgrades, as well as write new policies for the way employees utilize their electronic resources. The ultimate goal is to make the changes *before* the company is caught in an act of infringement.

The SPA offers a Fax-On-Demand service by calling 800-637-6823. It also offers the opportunity to report Internet piracy by calling 800-388-7478 (the Anti-Piracy Hotline), or by sending e-mail to piracy@spa.org.

Scanners

A scanner reproduces a photograph or other image in near perfect detail, then stores it for future use. More importantly where copyright is concerned, scanning technology gives the user the ability to use an image without decreasing quality. Images can be used over and over—and even altered. And all this can be done at no cost to the owner of the scanner!

In reality, the cost of this use could be greater than the user imagines. By reproducing, distributing or adapting a copyrighted image without permission, the user may have infringed on three of the five exclusive rights granted to copyright holders in Section 106 of the Copyright Act of 1976 (see Chapter 2). Some users may claim that their use of an image can be considered fair use. However, the copyright holder may not consider the use "fair."

Lotus v. Borland

Court cases involving software infringement are breaking new legal ground. The computer industry is hungry for legal precedents that will provide guidelines for future strategic planning and operational decision-making. One case originally filed in 1990 reached the U.S. Supreme Court early this year. Unfortunately, the 4-4 deadlock failed to provide a clear precedent for future cases.

In 1990, Lotus Development Corporation filed an infringement suit against Borland International Inc. Lotus, creators of the popular Lotus 1-2-3 spreadsheet program, claimed that Borland had "stolen" the "user-interface" from its spreadsheet and used it for its own spreadsheet program, called Quattro Pro. Borland never claimed that it had not taken the commands used by Lotus 1-2-3—only that the interface was not protected by copyright.

The U.S. District Court in Boston awarded Lotus $100 million in damages, finding that the interface was a form of "original expression" and, therefore, protected by copyright law. But Borland's victory came in 1995 when the U.S. Court of Appeals for the First Circuit overturned the District Court's ruling, finding that Lotus's menu-command hierarchy was akin to the buttons used to operate a VCR and was an uncopyrightable method of operation.

The case reached the U.S. Supreme Court. Ultimately, the court handed down the following opinion: "The judgement of the United States Court of Appeals for the First Circuit is affirmed by an equally divided court." The Justices had let the ruling of the lower court stand, thereby denying protection for Lotus. However, the 4-4 vote, which included no written explanation, failed to establish any course for future cases.

Scanning and the Internet

Not only can images be scanned and reproduced perfectly, but with the Internet, the images can be distributed around the world with the touch of a key. A quick scan of personal home pages reveals example after example of potential copyright infringement. Images ranging from Cindy Crawford to Dilbert to Winnie the Pooh are used, virtually always without regard to copyright. There are thousands of pages dedicated to particular celebrities or other interests, such as the "Babe of the Day" page maintained by one Internet user.

When the designer of one such page was e-mailed and asked if he had given any thought to copyright, he replied that he had gotten all of the pictures on his site from the Internet and posted them on the Internet, and if anyone ever asked him to remove them, he would do so gladly. A laudable sentiment to be sure, but a clear case of copyright infringement nonetheless.

Scanned images are subject to copyright law. As with copies made on a photocopier (see Chapter 10), or reproduced in any other fashion, using scanned images without the permission of the copyright holder may constitute infringement. When in doubt, ask the copyright holder. See Appendix A for a list of organizations that can help you find the copyright holders for photographs. For online information about the issue of image delivery and the Internet, visit the Copyright Website at www.benedict.com.

Online services

When people subscribe to an online service, then commit copyright infringement on their home page, does the service bear any responsibility? In recent years, several court rulings have said that providers of online services are responsible if copyrighted material is stored or distributed on their system.

One company that has taken the issue of copyright very seriously is Playboy Enterprises. Perhaps more than most copyright holders, Playboy falls victim to copyright infringement. You don't have to search too far on the Internet to find illegally scanned images from Playboy magazine. The company has made a concerted effort to fight back, bringing suit in 1993 against the proprietor of an online service that allowed users to store and distribute copyrighted images from Playboy (*Playboy Enterprises v. Frena*). Even though the service provider claimed to remove illegal images whenever he was aware of them, he was held liable for copyright and trademark infringement, as well as unfair competition.

A similar suit was won by Sega Enterprises, Ltd., the manufacturer of video games and systems. Sega sued an online service provider that had loaded Sega games on its system and made them available for its members to use and copy.

America Online, a major online service provider, has attempted to inform and educate its members about the dangers of copyright infringement, particularly in the creation of home pages. AOL uses its Web Page Toolkit to make home page creators aware that online images are subject to copyright law. There are also independent services that review home pages for those who are concerned about copyright violation.

E-mail

Electronic mail, or e-mail, has become the fastest-growing mode of communication since the cellular phone. The Electronic Messaging Association estimates that one billion e-mail messages were sent each month during 1995. As with most new technologies, e-mail can be both an asset and a liability to users. On the plus side, e-mail is a cost-efficient, extremely fast (compared to traditional mail, which some refer to as "snail mail"), and relatively private way to transfer information between parties.

On the other hand, e-mail users must turn on their computers and log on to an online service in order to retrieve messages. Users also must remember to save messages, or print them, if they want to keep them. And, recipients of e-mail messages must resist the temptation to forward private messages to others, or they may be in danger of committing copyright infringement.

Copyright enters the picture when a person receives an e-mail message, then uses the convenient "forward" feature that comes with most e-mail services. This feature allows an e-mail user to send a message to others, or post the message to one of many collections of messages grouped by subject, such as "usenet" groups. A message can be sent in its entirety, along with added comments from the person doing the forwarding. However, the ease of sending messages to others doesn't make it a legal practice.

According to existing copyright law, e-mail messages fall into the category of literary works. Literary works are described in the copyright law as "works other than audio visual works, expressed in words, numbers, or other verbal or numerical symbols or indicia, regardless of the nature of the material objects, such as books...tapes, disks or cards in which they are embodied."

E-mail messages clearly fit the above criteria. A key question still being debated is whether creating an e-mail message constitutes putting it in "fixed form" (one of the requirements, along with originality, for a work to be copyright-protected). Because most messages that are sent remain on the sender's hard drive (at least temporarily), it appears that they would be considered to be in fixed form.

The most important thing is that, as with letters, the copyright remains with the author of the message. The sender owns the copyright on the words; the recipient owns the physical space the message takes up on his or her hard drive, or the toner and paper if a hard copy of the message is made.The recipient does not have the right to copy, publish, or otherwise distribute the contents without permission. So, if someone sends you an e-mail message without giving you explicit permission to copy the message, refrain from passing it on to your mailing list or posting it to a newsgroup. Doing so could constitute copyright infringement.

Multimedia and CD-ROM

The possibilities of CD-ROM and other electronic publishing seem almost endless. You can include photos and other still images, music clips, spoken words, even video clips—not to mention good old-fashioned text. But as endless as the possibilities may seem, so are the copyright concerns for multimedia publishing.

Now, if you want to expose your audience to the inspiring words of Martin Luther King Jr.'s "I Have a Dream" speech, you are no longer limited to presenting the speech only in written form. You can produce your work electronically. With the CD-ROM version, your "reader" not only sees the text of the speech, he or she can *hear* the words spoken. Maybe he or she can even see Dr. King deliver the speech. You can even add accompanying music, narration, and other images to make the effect of the message more dramatic. There is no limit to your creativity!

Unfortunately, there *is* a limit to your ability to deliver information—and that is copyright law. Each technological breakthrough adds a new copyright factor for multimedia developers to consider. To present Dr. King's speech in a multimedia format, you need to request the rights to use more than just the words of the speech and photo to accompany the text. You now need rights for the sound recording, the video image, any music you have added, any additional images you put in, and so on.

I paid for it—why can't I use it?

Part of the confusion over copyright and multimedia stems from the fact that information (images, music clips, etc.) is so easily accessible. CD-ROM collections of photos, graphics, even parts of musical scores can be found for very reasonable prices at any software or large office supply store. However, as with images found on the Internet, the ease of access to the material, even if you have purchased a collection, does not guarantee that you can use them in your own multimedia project, especially if you intend to sell it.

Software packages, including CD-ROM collections, contain various levels of licensing agreements and should always be read carefully by the purchaser. In other words, you're not just buying the "information," you're buying the rights to use the information a specific way, and sometimes the way you can use the information is extremely limited by the licensing agreement.

Multimedia Developers Be Aware!

Multimedia developers should pay attention to the following items when developing their products:

♦ Contracting with employees, independent contractors and consultants for the creation of your multimedia work.

♦ Avoiding infringement of others' intellectual property rights.

♦ Obtaining licenses to use content owned by others.

♦ Complying with union rules.

♦ Contracting for sale or distribution of your work.

♦ Protecting the intellectual property rights in your multimedia work.

(cont.)

These legal issues are frequently as important to a multimedia developer as the technological and creative issues involved in multimedia projects. A multimedia developer who fails to obtain the necessary rights to use material owned by others can incur liability for hundreds of thousands or even millions of dollars in damages.

Example: Productions, Inc., created an interactive multimedia training work, "You Can Do It." The script was written by a freelance writer. "You Can Do It" includes an excerpt from a recording of Julie Andrews singing "Climb Every Mountain." It ends with a photograph of Lauren Bacall shown above the words, "Good Luck."

In this example, if the Productions staff did not obtain permission to use the recording of "Climb Every Mountain" or the photo of Lauren Bacall, "Do It" infringes on three copyrights: the copyright on the song, the copyright on the Julie Andrews recording of the song, and the copyright on the photograph. In addition, the photograph violates Ms. Bacall's rights of publicity and privacy. If Productions did not acquire ownership of the script from the freelance writer, the company does not have clear title to "Do It" and distribution of "Do It" may infringe on the writer's copyright in the script.

From *Multimedia Law Handbook* by J. Dianne Brinson and Mark F Radcliffe. Copyright © 1994 by J. Dianne Brinson and Mark Radcliffe. Reprinted by permission.

The bottom line for multimedia developers is be aware—be *very* aware! Understand that each component of your product may be subject to the U.S. copyright law. Contact a copyright attorney or copyright professional to be certain that all your rights and permissions are in order. What you haven't checked out could prove to be a costly oversight.

Summary

With new technology comes a variety of copyright concerns. Can copyright law keep up? Should software and other new media be viewed in the same way as a bound book? Or is the law technology-neutral and completely adequate to address the copyright issues of the digital age? Here are some important issues to keep in mind:

- Even though it may be easy to copy a software program onto many different computers or to make copies, the licensing agreement that comes with the program describes exactly the rights purchased with the program. Using the software in any other way can constitute infringement. Review carefully all licensing agreements.

- Schools and businesses are finding that site-licensing can offer cost-savings and convenience when multiple copies of a software program are required.

- The Software Publishers Association is an excellent resource for education and awareness of copyright issues related to software.

- Scanning a copyrighted image and distributing it without the permission of the copyright holder can constitute infringement. The fact that it's easy and that many others are doing it won't hold up well in an infringement suit.

- Online service providers may be held liable if they knowingly allow copyright infringement to occur on their systems. Consequently, the major providers are making efforts to educate and inform members about the appropriate uses of copyrighted material on home pages.

◆ E-mail messages are protected by copyright in the same way as letters (see Chapter 9). The copyright of an e-mail message belongs to the creator of the message. Distributing the message without the permission of the rights holder can constitute infringement.

◆ If you are developing a multimedia CD-ROM, be aware of all the rights that may be involved, including, music, print, audio, and still image.

As with any software package, a CD-ROM collection of clip art, photos, or music clips will include a license that clearly spells out what rights were purchased with the product, and how you can legally use the material contained therein.

10

Photocopying

Our lives were forever changed in 1960—with the introduction of the Xerox 914 photocopier. The impact has been tremendous: Businesses and organizations have been able to make copies of important materials—whether one-page fliers or 100-page reports—for employees, clients, customers and others—quickly and with little cost.

But where does the convenience and affordability cross the line into copyright concerns? While you may have to make your own interpretations in some cases, the copyright law does have some specific guidelines.

Personal use

You see a recipe for cranberry muffins in a magazine at the library. You'd like to add the muffins to your holiday menu. You don't have time to copy the recipe by hand or commit it to memory. You take the magazine to the copy machine, deposit your coin, push the button and put the copy in your purse.

Did you commit copyright infringement? Probably not. The folks at *Ladies' Home Journal* are not out to sue every reader who has copied one of the magazine's pages for personal use. But, let's say you test the recipe, and discover it makes the best muffins you've ever tasted. You make 50 copies and insert them in your Christmas cards to friends and relatives.

You now decide to write an article for your local paper on the holiday's best recipes and you include the muffin recipe. A literary agent reads your article, gives you a call and asks if you have ever thought of writing a book, a collection of favorite holiday recipes. You include the recipe in your book.

Have you committed copyright infringement? What started out as a single copy for personal use has now grown to 50,000 copies, distributed worldwide, for which you have received compensation. *Ladies' Home Journal* would have a good case against you.

At what point has copyright infringement taken place in this example? When you received a royalty on the cookbooks? When you included the recipe in the newspaper article? When you made 50 copies and distributed them to friends? Unfortunately, the law provides no absolute answers. What is clear, though, is that the copyright owner of a work is granted by law the exclusive right to reproduce or make a copy of the work and the exclusive right to distribute the work. The burden of interpreting the law in each case rests upon the individual making the copy.

We have all made photocopies for our own personal use—whether it's a newspaper article for a research paper, a humorous cartoon we stick on the refrigerator, or a recipe. Whenever we photocopy copyrighted material, it is important to consider the four factors of fair use:

♦ *Purpose and character of the use.* Are you making the copy of an article for research for a term paper? Are you making copies of a map to include in 100 wedding invitations? Or are you copying the map to accompany a travel article to be published in a national magazine?

♦ *Nature of the material.* Will you be making copies of your sister's diary? Or the sheet music for "I Hope I Get It" from *A Chorus Line*? How about your friend's home page on the World Wide Web? Or a love letter from an admirer?

♦ *Amount and substantiality of the material.* Are you copying a chapter from a 300-page book? Or just a paragraph?

♦ *Market effect of the use.* Are you copying the Sunday crossword puzzle from *The New York Times?* Are you making copies of an article (rather than purchasing reprints) from *Inc.* magazine to pass out at a national sales conference? Are you copying a software manual for your entire staff rather than buying additional copies?

Archival copying

Does photocopying an article and keeping it on file for future use constitute infringement? This question of archival photocopying tested fair use when, in 1985, six publishers— American Geophysical Union, Elsevier Science Publishing, Pergamon Press, Springer-Verlag, John Wiley, and Heydon— brought suit against oil giant Texaco, Inc.

The suit, which had originally been filed as a class action suit on behalf of 1,600 technical and scientific publishers, claimed that Texaco's research scientists photocopied copyrighted journal articles and placed them in files for future research with no compensation to the copyright holders.

Lawyers for Texaco argued that the photocopying done by their employees was fair use, citing in particular the following:

♦ The photocopying constituted a goal of copyright—to advance and promote arts and sciences.

♦ Texaco was not a publisher; no profit was made from the photocopying because they didn't republish the material or sell the articles.

The case was in the courts for seven years before U.S. District Judge Pierre Leval of the United States District Court in New York handed down his decision on July 12, 1992. Although Judge Leval acknowledged the fair use arguments, he found that the ultimate purpose of the Texaco research was "to create new products and processes for Texaco that [would] improve its competitiveness and profitability." He found Texaco liable for copyright infringement in the case of *American Geophysical Union v. Texaco, Inc.*

In December 1992, the Second Circuit accepted Texaco's appeal. A number of library associations filed briefs in support of Texaco's appeal, prompted by their concern about the effect the Texaco decision might have on not-for-profit libraries. The decision, however, was upheld in 1994: Archival corporate photocopying can be considered copyright infringement. Corporate copiers should carefully evaluate the need to obtain permission and compensate the copyright holder before proceeding.

How does one obtain the permission and compensate the copyright holder? The Copyright Clearance Center in Danvers, Mass., is a primary source for a photocopying license. The not-for-profit licensing organization represents more than 9,000 publishers. For more information on CCC, call 508-750-8400 or contact it through the Internet at http://www.copyright.com.

Classroom copying

More than 20 years ago, the U.S. Copyright Office adopted these fair-use guidelines for classroom copying of books and periodicals in not-for-profit educational institutions:

Single copying for teachers

A teacher may make a single copy of any of the following for scholarly research, use in teaching, or in preparation to teach a class:

♦ A chapter from a book.

♦ An article from a periodical or newspaper.

♦ A short story, short essay, or short poem.

♦ A chart, graph, diagram, drawing, cartoon, or picture from a book, periodical, or newspaper.

Multiple copies for classroom use

A teacher may make multiple copies of the items listed previously (not to exceed more than one copy per pupil in a course) provided that all of the following criteria are met:

♦ The amount of the material copied is brief.

♦ The copying is done spontaneously.

♦ The cumulative effect test is met.

♦ Each copy includes a copyright notice.

What is considered brief?

♦ **Illustrations**. One chart, graph, diagram, drawing, cartoon, or picture per book or per periodical issue.

♦ **Poetry**. A complete poem of 250 words or less that is printed on no more than two pages or an excerpt of no more than 250 words from a longer poem.

♦ **Prose**. A complete article, story, or essay of less than 2,500 words, or an excerpt up to 1,000 words of 10 percent of the work, whichever is less, but in any event a minimum of 500 words.

♦ **Special works**. No more than two pages and not more than 10 percent of the words from works that combine language with illustrations and have less than 2,500 words.

What is spontaneous?

The copying must be the idea of the teacher (not the administration), and the decision to use the work must come so close to classroom time that there is not time enough to get permission from the copyright holder.

What is a cumulative effect?

The copying of the material is for only one course in the school. Not more than one short poem, article, story, essay, or two excerpts may be copied from the same author, nor more than three from the same collective work or periodical volume during one class term. There are no more than nine instances of multiple copying for one course during one class term.

Course packet publishing

The Kinko's case

For years, professors had created their own course materials for students rather than use traditional classroom texts. Course packets—custom packs that typically include copyrighted material—allowed the professors an educational freedom. That freedom suddenly came to an end following two important cases.

In March 1991, the United States District Court for the Southern District of New York found Kinko's Graphics Corporation guilty of copyright infringement for its practice of copying and selling for profit, without permission or payment of a royalty fee, customized anthologies of excerpts from books and articles that professors selected for their teaching curriculum. The suit was brought by seven publishers—led by Basic Books.

Following the ruling, the demand for producing course packets remained strong. Many college bookstores and copy shops took on the role of course packet publisher. Bookstore employees who had previously been ringing the register or placing book orders found themselves thrown into the thick of the permissions process. Almost overnight they had to learn about copyright pages, public domain, and the doctrine of fair use—all with little or no knowledge of the law with which they were expected to comply.

Professors had to accept the fact that the materials they used were no longer free—royalties for copyrighted material had to be paid. The cost of a course packet went up considerably (more than 50 percent) to cover permissions fees, much to the dismay of the customer, the student.

The court decision was a two-edged sword for publishers. While protecting the reproduction and distribution rights of their copyrighted works, publishers threw a monkey wrench into the already confusing permissions process. Publishers were deluged with requests for instant permission from inexperienced requesters. It has taken several years since the Kinko's case to get the course packet permissions process more manageable. And while professors are still upset that they have to pay for permissions, they are learning to comply with the law.

Michigan Document Service

Another case is still making waves. On Feb. 12, 1996, the U.S. Court of Appeals for the Sixth Circuit—the highest court to rule on this issue to date—ruled that Michigan Document Services was not infringing on the copyrights of three publishers who had brought suit against the copy shop in 1992 for photocopying copyrighted material for course packets. (*Princeton University Press v. Michigan Document Services.*) This ruling overturned a June 1994 decision that favored the publishers.

On April 9, 1996, the U.S. Court of Appeals for the Sixth Circuit agreed to rehear the copyright infringement suit against MDS. While the case was originally heard by a three-member panel, it was then reheard by the entire court. Both parties involved in the case have been ordered to provide supplemental briefs and present their arguments again. In November 1996 the entire Sixth Circuit vacated the decision of the three-judge panel and affirmed the District Court decision that MDS infringed the plaintiff's copyright. However, the court concluded that MDS did not willfully infringe the plaintiff's copyright.

Libraries and photocopying

Other institutions are faced with similar issues regarding photocopying. Libraries have had to find a delicate balance between their patrons' demands for instant information and observance of the copyright law.

Section 108 of the Copyright Act addresses reproduction by libraries and archives. Libraries are permitted to reproduce and distribute no more than one copy of a work as long as the following criteria are met:

♦ The copy becomes the property of the user.
♦ The copy must contain a notice of copyright as specified in Section 108(a).

♦ The library must have no reason to believe that the patron's use is not a fair use of the material.

♦ The library prominently displays, at the place where orders for copies are placed and on the order form itself, a warning in accordance with a regulation developed by the Register of Copyrights.

For more information on libraries and copyright issues, see Chapter 13.

Copy shops

Ask a clerk to make several copies of an article from *Newsweek* and your attention may be directed to a sign posting a copyright warning. Or ask the clerk to enlarge a Far Side cartoon into a poster and you may be asked to show your letter of permission. Many copy shops have strict policies—perhaps not so much out of respect for copyright as out of fear of litigation. Nonetheless, having the patron make the copy at the self-service machine takes away the liability of the shop. Remember in the Kinko's case, it wasn't the professors who were sued, but rather the copy shop.

Summary

As fast and easy as photocopying may be, the right to reproduce material is one of the exclusive rights of a copyright holder. Here are some important things to remember when photocopying copyrighted material.

♦ Making a single photocopy of an article, a poem or a recipe for your personal use is generally accepted as fair use. But the more copies you make for more people, the greater your risk of committing infringement.

- In the Texaco case, a federal appeals court decided that archival photocopying for business use constituted copyright infringement.

- The U.S. Copyright Office has adopted a set of fair use guidelines for classroom copying. Specific rules must be followed for both single copying for teachers and multiple copies for classroom use.

- While professors at one time enjoyed the freedom to create their own "custom books" via photocopying, the Kinko's and Michigan Document Service cases found the practice to be an act of copyright infringement. Course packets are still frequently used in the academic environment, but reprint permission from copyright holders is now required.

- Section 108 of the Copyright Act of 1976 provides specific guidelines for photocopying by librarians for patrons.

- As a result of the aforementioned cases, copy shops have become increasingly sensitive to copyright infringement. The responsibility is now placed with the consumer, as most copy shops will not allow their staff to make copies of copyrighted material without written permission from the copyright holder.

11

Using Other People's Property

Imagine a term paper without footnotes or references—a paper based purely on the opinion of the author. Think about how would you feel if you were looking through an art book that merely wrote about the artists and *described* the works of fine art they had created—no reproduction of "The Blue Guitarist," for example, to depict Pablo Picasso's Blue Period.

There would be a void, something missing. You would probably feel unsatisfied. Wouldn't you be curious about how the author of the term paper came to the conclusions he or she presented in his paper? Or how Picasso's sadness came through in his art? There would be no depth to the presentations. Using other people's work to explain our own gives our work credibility and substance. By incorporating other materials we add dimension.

Let's say you have been selected to give a speech at a fund-raising event for Sudden Infant Death Syndrome. You've found an article written by a mother who recently lost her son to SIDS. You want to use something from the article in your speech. It will be more powerful than the lists of statistics you have gathered. It might bring the room to tears.

You have some choices if you want to include the material. You could *paraphrase* the article—tell in your own words what the mother went through. You could *plagiarize*—tell her story as if *you* had written the article—that *you* had lost a son. Or you could *request permission* to include passages from the article and let the mother tell her story in her words.

Paraphrasing

Paraphrasing is a way to share someone else's story without infringing upon or "stealing" their intellectual property. The key to paraphrasing is relating the material in your own words. If someone held the original material and yours next to each other, there should be a distinct difference in the way each is written. For example, if you were preparing the SIDS speech, you might say, "A mother of a 9-month-old son whom she recently lost to SIDS says that the hardest thing for her to accept was that she might have been able to save him if she had just been there when he was sleeping." None of these words are taken directly from the article.

Plagiarism

The term comes from the Latin word *plagium,* meaning kidnapping. It has been said that the Roman poet Martial accused those who stole his words of "plagium." Plagiarism is the act of taking someone else's ideas, writings or intellectual property and presenting them as your own.

Plagiarism can be a costly act. Think of what plagiarism did for Senator Joe Biden's presidential bid in 1988 when he borrowed a moving soliloquy from British Labor Party leader Neil Kinnock with no attribution to Kinnock. The act of plagiarism cost him any hope of becoming president.

Be aware that plagiarism and copyright infringement are two distinct acts. Plagiarism is wrong based on ethical rather than legal definitions. Copyright infringement is an illegal act. While an act of plagiarism may also be an act of copyright infringement, only the copyright infringement is punishable by law (as a general matter, infringement isn't a criminal act—*civil* liability may be imposed). If a student takes the words of Thomas Jefferson—which are in the public domain—he or she is guilty of plagiarism but not copyright infringement.

Permission

If you borrow material directly from another source and it is not in the public domain (see Chapter 3) and the use of the material cannot be considered fair use (see this chapter as well as Chapter 4), then you will probably need to request permission. Using copyright material without permission, even if you attribute it to the proper source, can be copyright infringement. For example, if you were to excerpt parts of the article on SIDS and include them in an article you were writing on the grieving process—and you didn't get permission—the author may have a good case for copyright infringement.

Whenever you borrow material from another source, think about the way you are using it. Have you merely re-stated the material in your own words? Have you forgotten to cite your source? Does it appear as though this was your idea or words? Will you be using exact words from the material? Be aware that the *only* way to safely use copyrighted material is to request and get permission. A common mistake many people make is to assume that citing the source is all that is necessary.

Using Copyrighted Materials Safely

Plagiarism, infringement, ethical violations, lawsuits. At times it may seem nearly impossible to use copyrighted material without committing some type of legal offense. Here's an overview of the safest ways to use the works of others:

1. **Paraphrase.** Put it in your own words. Read the material, even take notes, and then write it in your own words.
2. **Find similar material in the publicdomain.** Find something out of copyright or published by the government which would be in the public do main. You can borrow freely without danger of infringement.
3. **Get permission.** While copyright holders can say no, they frequently don't. In fact, many will be delighted to have their work exposed.

Material in the public domain

Material in the public domain is free for all to use in any way they wish to use it. You will need to consider the following questions to determine if the material is in the public domain. If the answer to any of the questions is yes, then the material is in all likelihood in the public domain.

♦ Has the copyright expired?

♦ Is the material from a U.S. government document, or from materials published by the Government Printing Office?

♦ Is the speech given by a public official as part of his or her job?

♦ Is the material common knowledge or common facts?

It is important that you carefully consider the material you want to use, keeping in mind the nuances of the law. Under the old law (pre-1978), copyright protection began upon publication with a valid copyright notice. That means that a poem by Emily Dickinson published in 1914 (more than 75 years ago) is not automatically in the public domain. Many of Emily Dickinson's unpublished poems were found in a trunk by a relative and not "published" until the 1950s when Harvard University Press released an anthology, *The Complete Poems of Emily Dickinson*, edited by Thomas H. Johnson.

Be cautious of old works that have been translated or retold when considering the copyright status. The translation or retelling may be in copyright and require permission. For example, *The Metamorphosis* by Franz Kafka was published in 1915 and is in the public domain. However, it was translated into English in 1948. That translation was registered, and copyright was renewed in 1975. Therefore, the translation is still in copyright.

Beware, also, of public domain works that have introductory material, editorial notes or changes. The new material added to the work may be in copyright. Consider the Riverside Shakespeare version of the play *Macbeth*. Although William Shakespeare wrote the play centuries ago, the copyright to the introduction and the footnotes is controlled by Houghton Mifflin, the publisher of the Riverside edition. If you are using any of the footnotes or introductory material, you will have to get permission.

If you have determined that the material you want to use is not in the public domain, your next step is to determine if you can claim fair use.

Can I claim fair use?

Fair use is without a doubt the most confusing aspect of copyright law. There are no absolute definitions in the

Copyright Act of 1976—only a set of guidelines. When determining if the use you are proposing is a fair use, you will need to hold it up to Section 107, the Fair Use Doctrine. Ask yourself the following questions:

♦ What is the *purpose and character* of my use?

♦ What is the *nature* of the material I want to use?

♦ *How much and how substantial* is the portion I want to use in relation to the work as a whole?

♦ What is the *effect* of my use on the market for or value of the work?

If you are using the photo of Whoopi Goldberg in a bathtub of milk taken by Annie Liebovitz to sell your new line of bathroom fixtures, you may want to reconsider moving ahead without getting permission. Ms. Liebovitz (and Ms. Goldberg, for that matter) may not think it would be fair for you to use the photograph for that *purpose*.

If you want to include passages from your sister's diary in a novel you are writing, you may find your sister quite distressed, simply due to the private *nature* of the diary.

If you are thinking of singing the first two verses of "Bridge Over Troubled Water" by Paul Simon and Art Garfunkel to market your bridge-building consulting company, you may find yourself in troubled waters. Two verses is a *considerable amount* of the famous song.

If you make 30 copies for your book club of Hemingway's short story "Hills Like White Elephants," you may find that publisher Charles Scribner's Sons could cite a loss of royalty income from the lost sales as the adverse *effect* the copying had on their property.

Caution should always be exercised before claiming fair use with certain forms of copyrighted material. Song lyrics, poetry and drama are especially sensitive because of their "compact expression." A line of poetry, for example, can be loosely equated to a chapter in a book. What may seem like a small amount of material is really quite substantial. Consider 55 words. While 55 words from the James Michener's *Alaska* is a small portion of the more than 300,000 words that make up the novel, 55 words of Robert Frost's poem "Stopping by Woods on a Snowy Evening" is a substantial amount of the work—more than half.

Beware! Anytime you adapt copyrighted material without permission you are taking a risk. Remember, the copyright law and the fair use doctrine are written in broad language and meant to be open to interpretation. The only true test of whether a use is fair would be determined in court. Would it be worth the time and money you would give up to defend your position in court? Even if you won? Give careful consideration before claiming fair use. When in doubt, don't. Ask for permission.

How to obtain permission

Once you have decided that the material you want to use is *not* in the public domain and you feel the use is not a fair use, you must obtain permission to use the material. The following steps need to be taken to obtain permission for copyrighted material:

- ◆ Locate the permission grantor.

- ◆ Send a letter that states very clearly what you wish to use and how you wish to use it.

- ◆ Allow enough time for a response—at least two to three months. Permissions departments are very busy.

- ◆ Follow the stipulations of the agreement you receive.

Locating the permission grantor

The permission grantor is the party who holds the granting rights for the copyrighted material. The granting rights are determined by the contractual agreement the copyright holder has with the publisher or producer of the work. For example, let's say you want to use a chapter from Stephen King's novel *It* as part of a book on writing. While King retains the copyright to all his novels, as is the industry standard for fiction writers, he probably has conveyed to his publisher, Viking Penguin, the publishing rights, one of which is the right to license others to make derivative works, such as your book on writing.

I don't envision Stephen King's mailbox filled with letters requesting permission to use his work. Mr. King has more important things to do with his time—such as write more books. Rather, a request for permission should be sent to the permissions department at Penguin USA, the division of Viking Penguin that controls the granting rights for Stephen King's work.

There are instances where the copyright holder does grant permission. Many freelance photographers and writers grant their own permissions. It just depends on their contractual arrangement.

Sometimes the permissions process can get very complicated. Sometimes you can't even find the copyright holder. What do you do in the case where you have tried and tried and come up with nothing? Let's say the essay you want to use came from a magazine published in the 1970s. The magazine is no longer published. Because rights are probably with the author, you try to locate the author, searching every possible resource available.

Can you use the material without permission? You *can* use the material without permission, but it is just that—*without permission*. The author could find his or her material in your book, then come to you to ask for compensation or take you to court. A record of a "good faith effort" in trying to obtain permission does not substitute for written permission.

There are many valuable resources available for trying to locate copyright holders. (See Appendix A.) Keep in mind also—there is no substitute for a helpful reference librarian!

Put your request in writing

Your request for permission must be in writing. Your letter should include the following information:

♦ Identify the exact material to be used. Let the grantor know what you intend to use. Mark any adaptations or excerpting clearly.

♦ Describe the work for which you are requesting the copyrighted material.

♦ Name of your publisher, organization, or school.

♦ Identify the format of your work. For example, hardcover text, magazine article, CD-ROM, video.

♦ Estimate the number of copies you intend to print or produce.

♦ Estimate the price you will charge per copy, if any.

♦ Mention the territory in which your materials will be distributed. Will it be limited to your church? Your city? State? Country? Or will the work be distributed worldwide?

♦ Identify your estimated publication or distribution date.

Always provide the permission grantor with two copies of your letter (one for his or her records and one to return to you) and include a place to sign and date the letter. The grantor may not always use your form, but you have made it much easier to provide a response. If you are sending a letter to an individual, provide a self-addressed stamped envelope. See Appendix C for a sample letter.

Allow enough time for a response

If you are expecting to hear back in a week or so, be prepared for disappointment. Although technology has allowed us to send a letter electronically around the world in a few seconds, that doesn't mean someone at the other end will respond as quickly. Keep in mind that some permissions departments receive up to 300 request letters per day. Many of the letters need to be researched to see who controls the rights. Rights can change at any time.

For example, a publisher sells a title to another company, and with it go the rights. A book goes out of print and rights revert to the author. Michael Jackson sells his rights in the Beatles songs. While some companies are set up electronically, not all departments have this information available at a key stroke. Publishers don't have a huge library at hand with every book they have ever published, just waiting for your request letter. Allow 3 to 4 months.

The copyright holder may say no

Can you believe that someone would really refuse permission for you to include their material in your project? Yes, it does happen and you may never know the reason. Perhaps, the estate of the copyright holder is in litigation at the time of your request, or the grantor does not allow any adaptations of the work, and you have made changes. It might be that the author feels his or her work has been used too much (it seems hard to believe but that was a reason given.)

The copyright holder has the right to refuse permission. A call might help to explain the reason, or to find a way to rework the material to make your use acceptable to the grantor. In any event, understand that the permission grantor may say no for any reason—or no reason at all.

One well-known author refused to have her work included in a collection of works from multi-cultural women writers. She had previously granted permission for her work to be included in such a collection. However, at the time of the request, she declined. She didn't state a specific reason, nor did she have to. She owns the rights to her own material. She can say no.

One of the best-known cases of a copyright holder protecting the ways in which his material was used is of J.D. Salinger, author of *Catcher in the Rye*. Salinger is a well-known recluse. He conducts the majority of his business through his literary agent at Harold Ober Associates.

In an incident reported by *The New York Times*, the loyalty of one of Salinger's fans was tested by copyright law. A college student named Stephen Foskett created a World Wide Web page dedicated to making excerpts of Salinger's writings available to "net-surfers" worldwide.

Chris Byrne of Harold Ober Associates e-mailed Foskett a succinct message that stated that J.D. Salinger never grants permission for his work to be used in any way, that he goes to great lengths to protect his rights as copyright holder, and that Foskett's page should be shut down immediately because it was a "flagrant violation" of Salinger's copyright.

Foskett countered with two lengthy e-mail messages citing fair use and describing the embarrassment Salinger would suffer if Foskett was forced to shut down the Web site. He also stated his great admiration and respect for Salinger.

Byrne, having stated his point, did not respond. Interestingly, Foskett came across a quote on the jacket of one of Salinger's books that stated Salinger's belief that "privacy and obscurity are a writer's sacred possessions." Having read these words from Salinger himself, Foskett decided to close the Web site.

No matter how much Stephen Foskett and those who accessed his Web site admire J.D. Salinger, and no matter how many copies of *Catcher in the Rye* and *Franny and Zooey* the Web site might help to sell, Salinger has the right to say no to any and all uses of his work, for any reason, or no reason at all. Regardless of the nobility of Foskett's motivation to close the web site, not doing so could easily have brought a suit from Salinger.

How much will permission cost?

Fees for reproducing copyrighted material can vary greatly. There is no absolute fee structure in the publishing industry.

Generally, the permission grantor will base his or her fee on the information you have given about the way you intend to use the material—number of copies, format of the work, territory of distribution, price, etc. The fee is also based on how much of the material you will be using—how many notes, length of footage (film clip), how many lines of poetry, number of words, etc. In the intellectual property business, the price for the property may not always be what the market will bear, but rather what the grantor wants to charge. Don't be surprised if a grantor charges a high fee for the property with no room for negotiation.

Follow the fine print

Contracts, by law, must be in writing. Therefore, the response to your request letter should be in writing. It is of utmost importance for you to read the agreement or license to make sure you have the rights you need, as well as to find out what you need to do to honor the contract.

For example, you may be asked to pay a fee on the signing of the agreement. You may be asked to include the credit line required, or to get additional approvals such as from the author who wrote the journal article you requested. You may only be given rights for North America.

Perhaps the most important requirement of the permissions agreement is the form of credit to be given to the copyright holder. This credit announces to the world who owns the property. Be sure you properly acknowledge the source. If the grantor does not provide you with a credit, follow the sample provided here:

> "How to Obtain the Rights to Copyrighted Material" by Cheryl L. Besenjak in *Copyright Plain and Simple*. Copyright © 1997 Cheryl L. Besenjak. Reprinted by permission.

Remember, grants of permission are legal, binding contracts. Read the fine print! And be certain to follow all the stipulations required.

Summary

The best way to understand the value of other people's property is to consider how you would feel if others were thinking of your property. Chances are, you'd want them to respect it, value it, and ask your permission before they used it or changed it.

Here are some keys to remember:

♦ When identifying a copyright holder, keep in mind that the publication in which a work appears is often not the rights holder for the work.

♦ The term *plagiarism* comes from the Latin "plagium," meaning kidnapping. An act of plagiarism may also be an act of copyright infringement, but it is not automatically so, if the material is not protected by copyright.

♦ The key to paraphrasing is relating the material in your own words. The safest way to paraphrase is to read the material, then put it away before writing about it (And don't peek!)

♦ If you decide you want to use someone else's copyrighted material, and it doesn't qualify as a fair use (see Chapter 4 and 12), you probably need to request permission from the copyright holder.

♦ Material in the public domain is free for all to use in any way they wish. Several key items to consider when determining if a work is in the public domain are:

• Has the copyright expired?

• Is the material from a U.S. Government document or agency?

• If the work is a speech, is it given by a public official as part of his or her job?

• Is the work considered common knowledge, or common fact?

♦ Be careful when claiming fair use of copyrighted material. You are still taking a risk by using material without permission.

♦ Once you have decided that you need to obtain permission, you should take the following steps:

  • Locate the permission grantor.

  • Send a letter specifically stating what material you wish to use and how you intend to use it.

  • Allow enough time for a response.

  • Follow all stipulations of the agreement you receive.

♦ Be prepared in case of a refusal. The copyright holder has the right to say no to your request, for any reason, or for no reason at all. You may want to have an alternative selection in mind.

12

Protecting Yourself From Infringement

The best way to avoid the hassles and expense of a copyright infringement suit? As we've reiterated throughout in this book, the wisest course of action is to get permission before using someone else's intellectual property.

But what if *you're* the one whose copyright has been abused? First, how do you know if your rights have been infringed? How can you prove infringement? And how can you fight back? That's what we'll explore in this chapter. And we'll cite several examples of infringement cases to illustrate the complexities as well as the consequences of copyright infringement.

Police your copyright!

Police your copyright! It's not uncommon for writers of children's literature to browse through the latest textbooks to see if their material is there and, if so, whether permission was obtained. Check out the World Wide Web. If you search for your name or titles of your work, what do you turn up? In addition to searching yourself, you will want to keep in mind the following:

◆ Understand your rights under the law.

◆ Put up that "no trespassing" sign—the copyright notice.

◆ Register your work. If you have to defend your copyright in court, you will have to prove you own the copyright by presenting a copyright registration.

Proving copyright infringement

Let's say you've discovered, through your travels on the World Wide Web or some other means, that your copyrights have been abused. Someone has reprinted several paragraphs of an article you wrote in a book. Or perhaps a photo you took turns up in a magazine spread. What can you do? What steps should you take to get credit, compensation or to avoid further infringement upon your rights?

1. Prove a valid copyright

Is the material original, creative, and in a fixed medium of expression? The best way to prove this is with the certificate of copyright registration for the work. If you take the case to court, you will need to bring this with you—it is the deed to your property!

2. Prove the work was copied, distributed, made into a derivative work, performed, or displayed

You will need to show these things:

◆ **Access.** Did the infringer have access to the material? Because published works are offered to the public, it is usually easy to prove access. For example, could the infringer have taken your book out of the library? Hear your song over the airwaves? Rented your video? Proving access to unpublished works is more difficult.

♦ **Similarity.** Is the copy significantly similar? Have words been copied verbatim? Are there identical characters in the story?

3. Prove that you took the "protected expression" of the work

What is original and unique to the work? How significant is the material? It may only be one line of poetry or a few bars of music.

Remedies for copyright infringement

1. Resolve it yourself

You have found someone copying your photo. You want the party to stop infringing on your copyright. You can begin with a friendly Cease and Desist Letter. By doing so, you are informing the party of your copyright. The letter (example shown on page 150) should include the following:

♦ Your name, business address, and telephone number.

♦ The name of your work, date of first publication, and the copyright registration of your work.

♦ The nature of the copyright infringement.

♦ A demand that the infringer cease and desist and pay for any damages.

♦ Require a response within a certain time period.

2. Work out a settlement

You hope your infringer will immediately comply with your request to stop infringing. It may not be that simple, but coming to an agreeable resolution is the hoped-for next step. Perhaps a license with a fee for the use would be agreeable. It would also be wise to include a reasonable

Cease and Desist letter

March 1, 1997

Ms. Ann Gardner, Publisher
How Does Your Garden Grow?
1234 Main St.
Hometown, IL 60123

Dear Ms. Gardner:

Recently I glanced through a copy of the Jan./Feb. issue of your
newsletter, *How Does Your Garden Grow?* I found that a sizable
excerpt from my article "Making the Most of Your Mulch" was
reprinted without my permission.

I own the copyright for the article which was written in March
1996 and was published in the June 1996 issue of *Better Homes
and Gardens*. The effective date of copyright registration is
April 15, 1996 and the registration number for the work is
TX-123456.

Since permission to reproduce and distribute copies of my work
has not been obtained, I consider your use an infringement on
my copyright. I demand that you cease and desist from selling
and/or distributing any more copies of the newsletter. In
addition, I ask that you compensate me in the amount of $100
for the use of the copies to date.

Please respond in writing to this letter by March 15.

Sincerely,

Rob Mather

Rob Mather

compensation for the use of your work. After all, you had to spend time "policing" your copyright. And remember, any settlement should be in writing, signed by both parties.

3. Go to court

You have not gotten the response you wanted from your notification. You feel you have to go to court to defend your copyright. What is involved in a lawsuit?

♦ Who can sue? The party that holds any of the exclusive rights or receives royalties from the property.

♦ Who is liable? Anyone involved in the right being infringed upon.

♦ How much time do you have to sue? Three years from the time of discovering the infringement.

♦ What are you entitled to? What can you demand of the infringer?

  • Injunction. An injunction is a court order requiring an infringer to stop publishing or distributing the work and to destroy all remaining copies.

  • Attorney fees. If you win your suit, the court may also deem it necessary for the defendant to pay your attorney fees and other costs of going to court.

  • Actual damages and infringer's profits. The plaintiff is entitled to be compensated for the actual money/royalties the infringement cost in lost sales and other avenues. This is not always easy to prove. The plaintiff is also entitled to the defendant's profits attributable to the infringement and that are *not* taken into account in computing actual damages.

- Statutory damages. These are established by copyright law. The plaintiff does not have to prove any loss but the work must have been registered with the Copyright Office. Amounts vary depending on whether the infringement is determined "innocent" or "willful." (See below.) Damages can be as low as $200 or as high as $100,000. Damages also may be remitted if the infringer was an employee of a nonprofit educational institution, library, or archive who reasonably believed the use was fair. It should be noted that the winning plaintiff may choose between actual damages and profits *or* statutory damages. S/he may *not* get both.

Innocent Infringement?

Is there such thing as innocent infringement? Maybe you should ask George Harrison. In 1970 he recorded the song "My Sweet Lord" on his album *All Things Must Pass.* Harrison was sued for copyright infringement by Bright Tunes Music Corp., owners of the copyright to the song "He's So Fine," which was written by Ronald Mack and performed by the Chiffons. Bright Tunes Music claimed that Harrison copied the melody of the song. Despite Harrison's defense of his innocence—that he did not knowingly copy the song—the court found Harrison guilty and concluded that Harrison may have unconsciously copied the tune. The court stated:

"His subconscious knew it already had worked in a song his conscious did not remember... That is, under the law, infringement of copyright, and is no less so even though subconsciously accomplished."

Summary

Copyright infringement can be costly—for the holder as well as the infringer. If you hold copyrights, it's important for you to defend your intellectual property just as you would your "real" property.

♦ One very important way to protect your copyright is to police it! Check the Internet for possible infringements.

♦ Put your "no trespassing" sign up—the copyright notice—and register your work.

♦ If you discover a copyright infringement, first try to resolve it by sending a cease-and-desist letter, and try to work out an agreeable settlement.

♦ If you can't work out a settlement, be prepared to take your case to court.

♦ To prove copyright infringement has taken place: prove a valid copyright, prove the work was copied, prove that the defendant took the "protected expression" of the work.

♦ If you win an infringement suit, you may be entitled to an injunction, actual damages, and infringer's profits or statutory damages, and attorney fees.

♦ Infringement can be innocent or willful. In either case, there are legal consequences. George Harrison lost just such a case when his song "My Sweet Lord" bore too much a resemblance to "He's So Fine," by the Chiffons.

13

Libraries and Educational Institutions

Although libraries and educational institutions are in the business of making information available, the very goals they strive to achieve can create copyright concerns. What copyright issues do libraries and educational institutions face? How do they pursue their mission and comply with the law at the same time?

Savvy library patrons are requesting fast-food-style service of library materials. After placing an order they want instant information. Librarians are eager to fulfill their mission to ensure access to information for all. But librarians have to look to the copyright law for guidance. In academic and public libraries alike, librarians must find the delicate balance between their patrons' demands for services with the appropriate use of copyrighted material as they develop policies for their institutions.

Fair use and document delivery

Document delivery can be described as the delivery of books or articles in the form of originals, photocopies, or electronic copies to a user upon request. Librarians often are asked to provide three types of document delivery services: photocopies, interlibrary loans, and reserve copies. The question facing librarians is: What is fair use in the library setting?

Section 108 of the U.S. Copyright Act addresses reproduction by libraries and archives. Answers to the fair use question can be found in this section of the law and in subsequent guidelines that have been developed in response to the law. Let's consider each area in more detail.

Photocopies

Who hasn't spent time in the library making photocopies? In Chapter 10 we talked about Kinko's Copy Centers and the legalities of copying. Does the law differ when it's a librarian doing the copying in a library setting? Section 108 permits certain libraries (the collections of the library must be open to the public or available to researchers not affiliated with the library's parent institution) to reproduce and distribute no more than one copy of a work as long as the following criteria are met:

♦ The library makes only a single copy of the same material.

♦ The library does not profit from its copying.

♦ The copy becomes the property of the user.

♦ The copy must contain a notice of copyright as specified in Section 108.

♦ The library must have no reason to believe that the patron's use is not a fair use of the material.

♦ The library must display prominently at the order desk and on the form a warning in accordance with a regulation developed by the Register of Copyrights.

Interlibrary loan

It is impossible for any library to have all the materials its patrons need at all times. For this reason, many library systems offer interlibrary loan service. It works like this: You request material from your library that it does not have. Your library searches the collections of other libraries within the system. The library finds the material you need and has it delivered—so that you can check it out. When you're done with it, you return it to your local library, where it is then returned to the original source.

The Interlibrary Loan Guidelines, negotiated by the Commission of the New Technological Uses of Copyrighted Works (CONTU), permit loan arrangements within limits. The "suggestion of five" guideline allows for the borrowing of up to five items from a copyrighted nonserial publication each year that the work is in copyright.

The CONTU Guidelines address the question of the extent to which a library may request copies of journal articles for its patrons from another library. The Guidelines suggest that the library is using interlibrary lending (actually document delivery) as a substitute for a subscription when, in any one year, it requests from other libraries more than five copies of articles from the same journal title (from issues published within the last five years). The borrowing library is required to certify that the request is within the guidelines and must retain records of such requests for up to three years.

Reserve copies

Many instructors assign readings to their students but find the materials are not readily available, or that the material may be a small part of a book, which the instructor doesn't want to require the students to buy. Rather than making multiple copies of the material, the instructor has the option of putting the material on reserve for students to read in the library.

The American Library Association Reserve Guidelines state that the amount of material that can be put on reserve by an instructor must be reasonable and that the number of copies should be reasonable. What is a "reasonable" amount? Considerations include the number of students in a class, the level of the class, the length of the assignment and the length of time before the assigned material must be read. ALA also states that a reasonable number of copies (for reserve) will in most instances be less than six.

The demand for delivery of copyrighted material by libraries is on the rise. James S. Heller, director of the law library and professor of law at The College of William and Mary, explains that librarians are feeling the "tension between providing good service to their patrons and respecting the rights of the copyright owners."

The Association of American Publishers, which strives to protect the exclusive rights of copyright owners granted under Section 106 of the Copyright Act, believes that the new technologies created after the CONTU agreements allow libraries to exceed the intention of the guidelines. In a statement on document delivery, the AAP criticizes libraries' "resource sharing" and cites primarily "the erosion of publishing revenues in this country, from: lost book and journal subscription sales, lost royalty income from licensing and lost new-product opportunities."

Libraries and technology

As the digital environment we now live in continues to develop and current law is being revised to accommodate the new technology, librarians and the publishing community may be at odds. While the issues of fair use in a digital age are being explored, Professor Heller reminds us that the current Copyright Act is "technology neutral." It makes no distinction between a "hard" or "electronic" copy.

Meanwhile, he suggests that librarians find a "safe harbor" in the law and the guidelines: Be certain that only one copy is provided for a patron (if a copy has been faxed or scanned, the copy created for faxing or scanning must be destroyed or deleted), stay within the CONTU guidelines of the "suggestion of five" for interlibrary loan materials, and observe the ALA Reserve Guidelines.

Educators and their special issues

Although the copyright law was written for "the advancement of learning in the arts and sciences," we must remember that the creation and distribution of information is big business. And whether an institution's goals are to advance learning, to further the public good or even to make money, respect for the law as it relates to intellectual property must be maintained. How do educational institutions walk this fine line?

Academic fair use

How can you advance learning if you hold tight the reins on material to learn from? How can you learn about dramatic irony if you can't quote from David Mamet or

Harold Pinter? How can you come to understand the intricacies of a fugue if you've never listened to a Bach concerto? How can you see the difference between false advertising and fair competition if you can't see and discuss advertisements?

Can a professor bring in a cigarette advertisement and point out to students how the advertiser is enticing children to want to try cigarette smoking? The teacher certainly has the right, through the First Amendment, to show the students the ad and talk about it. He or she may even have the right, according to the guidelines for classroom copying, to make and distribute a copy of the ad to students for this one class. But if he or she reprints the ad in a textbook, there is danger of infringement. Certainly, permission would be needed to include the ad in a textbook written and published for commercial gain. And permission is likely to be denied if the ad and company are shown in a negative light. It would be hard to prove academic fair use in the purest sense of the term in this case.

Let's consider another scenario: As part of a scholarly article, a professor compares Madonna's lyrics from her song "Material Girl" with those of "Diamonds are a Girl's Best Friend." An author now wants to include the article in an anthology for freshman rhetoric courses. The permissions researcher working on the project notifies the publisher that permission will need to be obtained for the lyrics included in the article.

The lyrics will no doubt be costly, and the researcher is concerned that the permission may be denied. She is a little concerned about the way that Madonna has been portrayed in the article. The editor does not see why she can't use the material without permission. The author of the article apparently did not get permission. And besides, she thinks, "What does Madonna care? She has plenty of money."

Of course, this is one of those tricky copyright situations. What may be considered academic fair use in a scholarly article, may not hold up in court when it comes to including the lyrics in a commercial college anthology selling 30,000 copies. Perhaps the biggest concern—would you want to go to court against Madonna and defend your position of fair use?

Multimedia fair use guidelines

"Multimedia," a now-common term in the classroom, refers to the use of more than one medium (print, audio, computer, video) to make a presentation. Students who were once limited to typewriter and carbon paper to create their research papers are now able to use video and computer equipment to create presentations that their parents would never have imagined possible. And educators have access to the same tools as students to make their own classroom presentations come alive.

But, as we have discussed repeatedly, the use of new technologies is accompanied by a new set of copyright concerns. Can a professor create a sampling of rock music to illustrate the history of rock and roll to his music appreciation classes? Can a student create a documentary on teen drug abuse for a sociology class, then sell the work to a company that produces educational videos?

A group of educators and copyright owners, meeting as the Fair Use Guideline Development Committee, has worked to address these issues. More than 50 organizations representing interest groups, including copyright users and copyright owners, brought their views to the table. Their goal was to address an important question: What is fair use in an educational multimedia environment?

The fair use doctrine suggests that greater rights (free speech, for example) may allow the use of copyrighted works when the use is "for purposes such as criticism, comment, news reporting, teaching (including multiple copies for classroom use), scholarship or research." (As noted earlier, four factors—purpose and character of the use, the nature of the work copied, the amount used, and harm to the copyright owner—will be considered in determining whether any such use is fair use.) But how far and to what extent can you interpret these words in the law? What is criticism? What is scholarship? Exactly what is educational multimedia fair use?

In 1996, the Educational Multimedia Fair Use Guidelines Development Committee put the finishing touches on such guidelines. The proposed guidelines have not been endorsed by many groups (including the major library associations) and, as of press time for this book, were being considered for adoption at the Conference on Fair Use (CONFU). Following are highlights from the guidelines:

Permitted educational uses

♦ *Educators* may perform and display their multimedia projects (which incorporate copyrighted works) as part of the curriculum-based instruction to students in face-to-face instruction, as assignments to students for directed self-study, or for remote instruction if the educational institution provides technology that limits access to students enrolled in the course and prevents making copies of copyrighted material. (The guidelines provide more limited use if copying cannot be prevented.) Educators can also use the projects in presentations to their peers at workshops or conferences and can be part of their professional portfolio.

♦ *Students* may perform and display their multimedia projects (which incorporate copyrighted works) in the course they were created for and may use them in their portfolio as examples of their academic work.

Limitations

♦ *Time.* A period of up to two years after the first instructional use with a class. Use beyond two years, even for educational purposes, requires permission from the copyright owners.

♦ *Portion:*

  • *Motion media.* Up to 10 percent or 3 minutes, whichever is less

  • *Text material.* Up to 10 percent or 1,000 words, whichever is less. An entire poem of less than 250 words, but no more than three poems by one poet, or five poems by different poets from an anthology. For poems of greater length, 250 words may be used but no more than three excerpts by a poet, or five excerpts by different poets in a single anthology.

  • *Music, lyrics, and music video.* Up to 10 percent, but no more than 30 seconds from an individual work. No changes can be made to the basic melody or the character of the work.

  • *Illustrations and photographs.* No more than five images by an artist or photographer. When using photos and illustrations from collective works, no more than 10 percent or 15 images, whichever is less.

  • *Numerical data sets.* Up to 10 percent or 2,500 fields or cell entries from a copyrighted database or data table—whichever is less.

Copying and distribution

Only a limited number of copies of the project can be made. No more than two use copies, only one of which can be placed on reserve for students to read or copy. One additional copy can be made for archival/preservational purposes.

When permission is required

The guidelines state that permission is required when the project is used for commercial reproduction and distribution, and also when the duplication and distribution of the projects exceeds the limitations outlined in the guidelines.

Accessing the guidelines

Full text of the guidelines, plus a list of those who developed and endorse the guidelines, is available from the World Wide Web through several addresses (www.axess.net/~lewis/fairuse/html is one), or you may contact the Consortium of College and University Media Centers.

Summary

As technology continues to make access to information from libraries and education institutions easier and faster, both must walk the fine line between providing what "consumers" want, while complying with copyright law. Here are some important points when considering copyright in a library or educational setting.

- ◆ Document delivery is described as the delivery of books or articles in the form of originals, photocopies or electronic copies to a user upon request.
- ◆ Guidelines permit instructors to put a limited amount of material on reserve for their students to review in the library.

- According to Section 108 of the copyright law, a librarian can make and distribute no more than *one* copy of a work, so long as a specific set of criteria are met.

- Copyright law is more liberal for those in a purely academic setting. However, the closer the use gets to being a profit-making venture, the greater the risk of an infringement suit.

- A set of guidelines to help students and educators in determining fair use when working with multimedia in an educational setting has been prepared.

14

The Future
of Copyright

The fundamental principles of copyright will remain constant. The law will continue to protect the rights of copyright holders. But as our world and technology evolve, our copyright law will continue to adapt to changing circumstances. Three areas can be identified as those that will have the most influence on the copyright landscape as we enter the 21st century:

- ◆ Technology.
- ◆ Education.
- ◆ Legislation.

Technology

Computers, software, modems and online services, multimedia, and other aspects of technology become more a part of the fabric of society each day. While technology has increased our ability to create, store and distribute information, it has also created copyright issues that were unimaginable to most people as recently as the late 1970s.

The greatest tool ever created for the transfer of information, the Internet is sure to be the center of much controversy in the coming years. The Internet makes it so easy to access, store, and transfer data worldwide that infringement can be committed with a single key stroke.

On one side of the debate are those who feel that the Internet is a tool to be used to allow free access to information for all people. Many see no need for regulating the distribution of information. There even exist on the Internet sites such as the "Anti-Copyright Website." Many articles have been written by so-called "copyright minimalists," about "copyright maximalists," who want to put a stop to the free flow of information now available to anyone with a computer and modem. (One interesting aspect of many of the articles critical of copyright law—they often end with a copyright notice!)

On the other side are those who feel that the Internet must be regulated in order to protect the value of intellectual property. These individuals are finding new ways to ferret out and put an end to the illegal copying and distribution of copyrighted material.

In Chapter 9 we discussed electronic rights and the use of scanned images without permission of the copyright holder. This practice is clearly employed by millions of computer users worldwide. However, this hasn't stopped copyright holders from identifying and attempting to shut down those sites that use material without permission.

For example, page 167 shows a notice that a representative of Playboy Enterprises, Inc., e-mailed to an Internet user who was maintaining a collection of copyrighted photos without permission.

The Internet is not the only temptation for potential infringers. It seems that each time you receive a new catalog from an electronics retailer, there is a new product that makes it easy for you to ignore copyright law. Take for instance, "Snappy," the computer chip that can "grab" a frame of any video or television show and create a "snapshot" for you to do with as you wish. The ad for "Snappy" makes no mention of the danger of using copyrighted images.

Where is Jenny?

From: Gene Snyder—Playboy Enterprises, Inc.

THIS IS YOUR SECOND WARNING

It has been brought to our attention that you have developed a Web site that illegally displays several images of Playmate Jenny McCarthy.

Playboy Enterprises, Inc., the publisher of PLAYBOY magazine, is the owner of the copyright and all right, title and interest in and to the material in our magazines. Any unauthorized reproduction of Playboy's copyrighted material constitutes copyright infringement.

Accordingly, we must request that you remove them from your Website.

Reproduced by Special Permission of Playboy magazine. Copyright© 1997 by Playboy.

You don't even need to be among the computer literate to see the effects of technology on copyright. You can just go to your local bakery. Imaging machines are now available that allow you to put any image directly onto a cake. So if you want Darth Vader, Bart Simpson, or Joe Montana on your child's birthday cake (all without permission of course), just bring in a photo and the bakery does the rest. When asked what they do about copyright, an employee of one bakery commented enthusiastically, "Oh, it copies just right!"

Education

Of course, one of the best ways to avoid infringement and increase awareness of the value of intellectual property is education. The Association of American Publishers (AAP) employs copyright professionals who conduct copyright education seminars and distribute educational materials.

There has also been discussion about an effort to begin teaching copyright in elementary schools. It is hard to imagine a better way to avoid copyright infringement than to teach children at a young age that intellectual property has value. Not only can children learn to respect the property of others, they may develop a deeper appreciation for what they create.

Copyright education is not limited to educational institutions and government seminars. Organizations such as the Software Publishers Association (see Chapter 9) have gone to great lengths to educate businesses and individuals about the danger of software piracy. The organization even offers the Certified Software Manager certification for those who have completed a comprehensive training program. The SPA makes an important point when discussing the economic benefits of copyright education and compliance: It can cost much less to get educated and comply with the law than to face an infringement suit.

As copyright continues to take on greater importance in our changing society, education should become more readily available.

Legislation

In 1995 Senator Orrin Hatch (R-Utah) and Senator Patrick Leahy (R-Vermont) introduced the National Information Infrastructure Copyright Protection Act in the U.S. Senate. At the same time, Congressman Carlos Moorhead (R-California) introduced identical legislation in the House of Representatives. The primary purpose of the bills, which were drafted after a two-year study by the Working Group on Intellectual Property, was to address one issue: "The protection of the content that moves on the national information infrastructure (NII)."

Before introducing the legislation, the Working Group put out a call for position papers from industry leaders involved in some way with electronic copyright issues. The response was overwhelming and the papers received offered perspective on the current law as well as recommendations as to what modifications might be made to keep the law current.

Senator Hatch has stated that "no manufacturer would ship his or her goods on a highway if his trucks were routinely hijacked." The Copyright Protection Act began "the process of designing the rules of the road for the information superhighway," according to Hatch. The proposed legislation targeted five areas of emphasis:

1. Transmission of copies.
2. Exemptions for libraries and the visually impaired.
3. Copyright protection systems.
4. Copyright management information.
5. Remedies.

During the year that followed the introduction of the bills, a variety of industry leaders testified during hearings for the proposed legislation, including Jack Valenti, president and CEO of the Motion Picture Association of America, John Bettis, president of the American Society of Composers and Publishers, and Daniel F. Burton, president of Novell, Inc., manufacturer of Netware software.

While lawmakers are not faced with major overhaul of the law, certain definitions in the law may need to be revised. The new technology has not created any new exclusive rights. Rather, the technology has challenged the meaning of terms such as "copies," "distribute," and "derivative works." Questions such as these have been raised:

♦ Is an e-mail message forwarded to another colleague a new "distribution?"

♦ Is a photo downloaded from an online service a "copy"?

♦ Is a faxed journal article a "copy"?

Response to the Copyright Act

Much of the debate over the issues raised by the Copyright Act has been conducted by the members of two major coalitions: The Digital Futures Coalition (DFC, whose members include the American Library Association, the American Historical Association, and the National Humanities Alliance.) and the Creative Incentive Coalition (CIC, whose members include the Association of American Publishers, the Motion Picture Association of America, and Microsoft, Inc.)

The positions of the two coalitions are relatively clear. The DFC is concerned that the proposed legislation goes too far in restricting access to information. The CIC strongly supports the legislation (and probably wouldn't mind if it went even further.)

The following excerpts from the two coalitions express their respective positions on the Copyright Protection Act. They also help to frame the ongoing debate over copyright protection on the Internet.

From "Statement of Members of the Digital Futures Coalition on H.R. 2441: The National Copyright Protection Act of 1995":

Our primary concern about H.R.2441 in its present form is that it fails to sustain the principle of balance, placing a nearly exclusive emphasis on the protection for copyrighted content, and doing sc at the expense of promoting innovation, privacy, education and public information access. This emphasis is a matter of both commission and of omission. Thus, we are concerned with the specific provisions of the bill itself—but we are equally concerned that it leaves many crucial issues, such as the place of "fair use" in the digital environment, unaddressed.

The provisions of H.R.2441 are not mere "minor adjustments" to the law of copyright... They are major proposals which—if enacted as written—will undermine the delicately calibrated balance of interests which characterizes our law of copyright. Once lost through piecemeal legislation, this traditional balance will not easily be restored. Our copyright system is a unique and complex web, and the various sections of the law are intricately woven together. Any legislation which focuses on only one part of the fabric, to the exclusion of others, runs the risk of unraveling the whole.

From a Creative Incentive Coalition Press Release—February 7, 1996. "Coalition Supports Digital Update of Copyright Laws" (Comments from Ken Kay, executive director of the CIC):

These hearings are an important step in making full use of the Internet...The Internet is already host to digitized versions of books, music, and even videos that can be downloaded or copied for free. Most of these creative works, however, are illegal copies and a prime example of what is stifling economic growth on the NII...Today a savvy Net surfer can find a good amount of bootlegged product for free.

This legislation will send a message to copyright owners that the government is reinforcing its longstanding commitment to copyright protection. It tells us that material transmitted via the NII will receive the same protection as material purchased in stores and elsewhere. This message will give our creative industries the assurance and confidence they need to reach their consumers via the NII.

Congress is also sending a clear signal to private industry that it is worthwhile to develop technology necessary to protect copyrights. And those who develop this technology can be assured that anyone who tries to undercut their technology will be in violation of the law.

Summary

As we look to the future, we can anticipate much debate, many new developments and a variety of changes in technology, education, and the law. But some things can be expected to remain constant:

♦ Intellectual property will continue to have value, and copyright holders will continue to fight to protect their property.

♦ No matter how much copyright education takes place, many people will continue to be unclear on the concept of intellectual property, and will, therefore, knowingly or unknowingly, commit copyright infringement.

♦ When making use of intellectual property, the closer you get to a profit-making venture, the greater your danger of an infringement suit.

♦ Copyright will continue to be big business.

♦ The debate over what is too little restriction and what is too much restriction over access to copyrighted material, on the Internet and elsewhere, will continue, and will surely grow louder.

♦ No matter what the circumstance, if you don't own the rights to copyrighted material, you can save yourself a great deal of money and time by finding out who holds the rights to the material you want to use, and getting their permission.

The debate over the Copyright Protection Act underscores the key themes of our journey through the basics of copyright law. On one hand, people want free and easy access to information. On the other hand, people want their property protected. Both are valid and defendable positions. In the end, whether the law is amended to reflect changes in society or technology, the best way to respect both positions is to become educated and to stay current on the issues related to copyright. Keeping your *Copyright Plain and Simple* on hand as a reference should help you do both.

Appendix A

Copyright Resources

Associations

The American Association of Publishers (AAP)
1718 Connecticut Ave. NW, #700
Washington, DC 20009
202-232-3335,
Fax: 202-745-0694

The American Society of Journalists and Authors (ASJA)
1501 Broadway, Suite 302
New York, NY 10036
212-997-0947,
Fax: 212-768-7414

The Copyright Society of the U.S.A.
1133 Avenue of the Americas
New York, NY 10036
212-354-6401

The National Writers Union
National Office East
113 University Place, 6th Fl.
New York, NY 10003
212-254-0279

The Software Publishers Association (SPA)
1730 M St. NW, Suite 700
Washington, DC 20036
202-452-1600,
Fax-on-demand service:
800-637-6823
Anti-piracy hotline:
800-388-7478

Books

All You Need to Know About the Music Industry, Donald S. Passman, 1994, Simon & Schuster.

The Copyright Book: A Practical Guide, Fourth Edition, William S. Strong, 1994, The MIT Press.

The Copyright Handbook: How to Protect and Use Written Works, Second Edition, Attorney Stephen Fishman, 1994, Nolo Press.

Copyright's Highway: From Gutenberg to the Celestial Jukebox, Paul Goldstein, 1994, Hill and Wang.

Does Your Project Have a Copyright Problem? A Decision -Making Guide for Libraries, Mary Brandt Jensen, 1996, McFarland.

Electronic Highway Robbery: An Artist's Guide to Copyrights in the Digital Era, Mary E. Carter, 1996, Peach Pit Press.

Kirsch's Handbook of Publishing, Jonathan Kirsch, 1996, Acrobat Books.

Kohn on Music Licensing, Al Kohn and Bob Kohn, 1996, Aspen Law and Business.

Libraries and Copyright: A Guide to Copyright Law in the 1990s, Laura N. Gasaway and Sarah K. Wiant, 1994, Special Libraries Association.

Multimedia Contracts 1996, Ladera Press.

The Multimedia Law and Business Handbook, J. Diane Brinson and Mark Radcliffe, 1996, Ladera Press.

The Nature of Copyright: A Law of User's Rights, L. Ray Patterson and Stanley W. Lindberg, 1991, University of Georgia Press.

Patent, Copyright & Trademark, Attorney Stephen Elias, 1996, Nolo Press.

The Public Domain Report Music Bible, Scott A. Johnson, Editor, 1996, Public Domain Research Corp.

A Writer's Guide to Copyright, Second Edition, 1996, Poets & Writers, Inc.

Newsletters

copyRights© Newsletter
from The Permissions Group
1247 Milwaukee Ave., Suite 303
Glenview IL 60025
800-653-7163, Fax: 847-635-6968, E-mail: PermGroup@aol.com
This bimonthly newsletter (six issues per year) is published by The Permissions Group and costs $89 per year. A free sample is available upon request.

The Public Domain Report
PO Box 3102
Margate NJ 08402
800-827-9401, Fax: 609-822-1638

The Public Domain Research Corp. publishes this monthly newsletter for $395 per year

Sub-Rights Letter
4 High Ridge Park
Stamford CT 06905
203-595-8250, Fax: 203-595-8251

For a $239 annual subscription, you get 24 issues of this newsletter from Intellectual Properties Council.

Organizations/institutions

California Lawyers for the Arts
Fort Mason Center
Building C, Room 225
San Francisco, CA 94123
415-775-7200
or 1549 11th St., Suite 200
Santa Monica, CA 90401
310-395-8893

The Copyright Clearance Center, Inc.
222 Rosewood Dr.
Danvers MA 01923
508-750-8400

Lawyers for the Creative Arts
213 West Institute Place, Suite 411
Chicago, IL 60610
312-944-2787

Poets & Writers Inc.
72 Spring St.
New York, NY 10012
212-226-3586
Providing publications, programs, and services for writers.

The U.S. Copyright Office
LM-455, Library of Congress
Washington, DC 20559-6000
Copyright Information Specialist, 202-707-6737
24-hour forms hotline, 202-707-9100

Volunteer Lawyers for the Arts
1 East 53rd St.
New York, NY 10022
212-319-2787

Rights clearance companies

BZ/Rights & Permissions, Inc.
125 West 72nd St.
New York, NY 10023
212-580-0615, Fax: 212-769-9224

Ferret Research
1517 N. Jackson St.
Waukegan, IL 60085
847-623-4744

The Permissions Group
1247 Milwaukee Ave, Suite 303
Glenview, IL 60025
847-635-6550; Fax: 847-635-6968
E-mail: PermGroup@aol.com

Web sites

American Society of Composers Authors and Publishers (ASCAP) http://www.ascap.com
Searchable database of ASCAP music titles, and a list of works to which copyright protection has been restored.

Carl UnCover http://www.carl.org/uncover
Searchable periodical database

Copyright & Fair Use (Stanford University Libraries) http://fairuse.stanford.edu

Copyright Clearance Center (CCC) http://www.copyright.com

Copyright Information Page (Univ. of Michigan) http://www.lib.umich.edu/libhome/copyright

The Copyright Website http://www.benedict.com

Corbis Corporation http://www.corbis.com
Searchable image database

Kohn on Music Licensing http://www.kohnmusic.com
A free resource for anyone who has questions about copyright law and licensing music for use and distribution.

Multimedia Law Website http://www.batnet.com/oikoumene/index.html
Multimedia law firms, software publications, multimedia organizations, U.S. Supreme Court decisions

National Writers Union http://www.nwu.org/nwu
Union of professional freelance writers

Software Publishers Association (SPA) http://www.spa.org
Conferences, networking opportunities, educational seminars, special interest groups

The U.S. Copyright Office http://lcweb.loc.gov/copyright

Appendix B

Sample Letters and Contracts

November 22, 1996

TPG #094CP97
(include on all correspondence)

Permissions Manager
W.W. Norton & Company, Inc.
500 Fifth Avenue
New York, NY 10123

Dear Permissions Manager,

I am preparing for publication with Career Press, Inc., the following title:

Copyright Plain and Simple by Cheryl Besenjak

Publication Date: 4/97
Edition: Trade
Binding: Soft
Number of Pages: 192

Proposed Price: $11.99
Market: U.S. and Canada
Language: English
First Printing: 5,000

We request nonexclusive reprint rights for the following:

Chapter 1, "How to Make the Most of Your Literary Works" from *Value Your Intellectual Property* by Avery Writer.

Please extend rights to all future editions, derivative works, and to special nonprofit editions for use by the handicapped.

For your convenience, you may indicate your approval by signing below and returning one copy of this letter.

Sincerely,

Cheryl L. Besenjak
Director

- -

Permission granted:

Date:_____   By:_____
                                          Authorized signature/title

Terms:_____   SS# or FID#:_____
                                               Required for payment

Credit line to read:_____

_____

_____

_____

_____

W • W • Norton & Company • New York • London

Contract No. 1529   Career Press, Inc.

Permissions Agreement

W.W. Norton & Company, Inc., grants the undersigned (hereinafter called the "applicant") nonexclusive license to use the following material (hereinafter called the "selection") subject to the terms on the reverse of this agreement:

Title: *Value Your Intellectual Property* by Avery Writer, "How to Make the Most of Your Literary Works" paperback $300

Credit Line: How to Make the Most of Your Literary Works," from *Value Your Intellectual Property* by Avery Writer. Copyright © 1996 by Avery Writer. Reprinted by permission of W.W. Norton & Company, Inc.

Territory: U.S./Canada
- -
This material is to be used, without change, in *Copyright Plain and Simple* (hereinafter called the work) by Cheryl Besenjak to be published by Career Press, Inc., in the English language only.

Paperback: Pages: 192   Printing: 5,000   Price: $11.99
Pub. Date: 4/1/97   Term of License: 10 years from
publication.   Total nonrefundable fee: $300

N.B. reference: 094CP97

                                   By:_____
_____
Signature of applicant   Frederick T. Courtright
                                   Rights and Permissions Manager
Date: _____   November 25, 1996

Cheryl Besenjak
The Permissions Group
1247 Milwaukee Ave., #303
Glenview, IL 60025

In consideration of permission to reprint the material specified on the reverse, the undersigned agrees that:

1. No deletion from, addition to, or other alteration in the text will be made without the written permission of W.W. Norton & Company, Inc.

2. Permission does not extend to material from other sources included in our publication, nor to any illustrations or charts unless specified on the reverse.

3. This grant is not transferable and is limited only to the specified edition(s) mentioned on the reverse.

4. No more than 10% of the applicant's work shall be composed of material quoted from works published by W.W. Norton & Company, Inc. and Liveright Publishing Corporation.

5. If any paperbound or other reprint, or revised edition is contemplated, further application for permission will be made to W.W. Norton & Company, Inc.

6. In the event a book club uses the applicant's work as a selection, dividend, or premium, the applicant will pay to W.W. Norton & Company, Inc., in addition to the fee set forth on the reverse, a sum that bears the same proportion to half the sum or sums paid by such book club as the W.W. Norton & Company, Inc. material bears to the entire contents of said volume, or $25, whichever shall be greater.

7. This grant is limited to the publication of the work in the language and territory listed on the reverse.

8. This grant will terminate without notice if any of the terms of this agreement are violated, or
      a. if the proposed work is not published within two years of the date hereof;
      b. if the published work remains out of print for six months;
      c. upon expiration of the term listed on the reverse.

9. The credit for each selection including the copyright notice as provided on the reverse will be printed in conformity with United States copyright law and acknowledgment will be given in every copy of the applicant's work on the copyright page or the first page on which such selections covered by this grant appear.

10. Grantee will pay W.W. Norton & Company, Inc., upon signing, but not later than 90 days from the date of this agreement, the fee specified on the reverse of this agreement, and return a copy of this agreement with payment, and send upon publication one copy of the applicant's work, Attention: Permissions Department.

11. This grant includes the right to sub-license, without charge, the publication or transcription into Braille or other aids for the handicapped, provided such editions are not sold or rented for a fee.

12. If the material is not used, grantee will advise W.W. Norton & Company, Inc. with a copy of this grant for cancellation.

Selected Copyright Law Statutes

§ 102. Subject matter of copyright: In general

- (a) Copyright protection subsists, in accordance with this title, in original works of authorship fixed in any tangible medium of expression, now known or later developed, from which they can be perceived, reproduced, or otherwise communicated, either directly or with the aid of a machine or device. Works of authorship include the following categories:

    (1) literary works;

    (2) musical works, including any accompanying words;

    (3) dramatic works, including any accompanying music;

    (4) pantomimes and choreographic works;

    (5) pictorial, graphic, and sculptural works;

    (6) motion pictures and other audiovisual works;

    (7) sound recordings; and

    (8) architectural works.

- (b) In no case does copyright protection from an original work of authorship extend to any idea, procedure, process, system, method of operation, concept, principle, or discovery, regardless of the form in which it is described, explained, illustrated, or embodied in such work.

§ 106. Exclusive rights in copyrighted works

Subject to sections 107 through 120, the owner of copyright under this title has the exclusive rights to do and to authorize any of the following:

- (1) to reproduce the copyrighted work in copies or phonorecords;
- (2) to prepare derivative works based upon the copyrighted work;
- (3) to distribute copies or phonorecords of the copyrighted work to the public by sale or other transfer of ownership, or by rental, lease, or lending;
- (4) in the case of literary, musical, dramatic, and choreographic works, pantomimes, and motion picture and other audiovisual works, to perform the copyrighted work publicly; and
- (5) in the case of literary, musical, dramatic, and choreographic works, pantomimes, and pictorial, graphic, or sculptural works, including the individual images of a motion picture or other audiovisual work, to display the copyrighted work publicly.

§ 106A. Rights of certain authors to attribution and integrity

(a) Rights of Attribution and Integrity. - Subject to section 107 and independent of the exclusive rights provided in section 106, the author of a work of visual art -
(1) shall have the right -
(A) to claim authorship of that work, and
(B) to prevent the use of his or her name as the author of any work of visual art which he or she did not create;
(2) shall have the right to prevent the use of his or her name as the author of the work of visual art in the event of a distortion, mutilation, or other modification of the work which would be prejudicial to his or her honor or reputation; and
(3) subject to the limitations set forth in section 113(d), shall have the right -
(A) to prevent any intentional distortion, mutilation, or other modification of that work which would be prejudicial to his or her honor or reputation, and any intentional distortion, mutilation, or modification of that work is a violation of that right, and

(B) to prevent any destruction of a work of recognized
stature, and any intentional or grossly negligent
destruction of that work is a violation of that right.

(b) Scope and Exercise of Rights. - Only the author of a work of visual
art has the rights conferred by subsection (a) in that work, whether or
not the author is the copyright owner. The authors of a joint work of
visual art are co-owners of the rights conferred by subsection (a) in that
work.

(c) Exceptions. - (1) The modification of a work of visual art which is a
result of the passage of time or the inherent nature of the materials is
not a distortion, mutilation, or other modification described in
subsection (a)(3)(A).

(2) The modification of a work of visual art which is the result of
conversation, or of the public presentation, including lighting and
placement, of the work is not a destruction, distortion, mutilation, or
other modification described in subsection (a)(3) unless the modification
is caused by gross negligence.

(3) The rights described in paragraphs (1) and (2) of subsection (a) shall
not apply to any reproduction, depiction, portrayal, or other use of a
work in, upon, or in any connection with any item described in
subparagraph (A) or (B) of the definition of "work of visual art" in
section 101, and any such reproduction, depiction, portrayal, or other
use of a work is not a destruction, distortion, mutilation, or other
modification described in paragraph (3) of subsection (a).

(d) Duration of Rights. - (1) With respect to works of visual art created
on or after the effective date set forth in section 610(a) of the Visual
Arts Rights Act of 1990, the rights conferred by subsection (a) shall
endure for a term consisting of the life of the author.

(2) With respect to works of visual art created before the effective date
set forth in section 610(a) of the Visual Artists Rights Act of 1990, but
title to which has not, as of such effective date, been transferred from
the author, the rights conferred by subsection (a) shall be coextensive
with, and shall expire at the same time as, the rights conferred by
section 106.

(3) In the case of a joint work prepared by two or more authors, the
rights conferred by subsection (a) shall endure for a term consisting of
the life of the last surviving author.

(4) All terms of the rights conferred by subsection (a) run to the end of
the calendar year in which they would otherwise expire.

(e) Transfer and Waiver. - (1) The rights conferred by subsection (a)
may not be transferred, but those rights may be waived if the author

expressly agrees to such waiver in a written instrument signed by the author. Such instrument shall specifically identify the work, and uses of that work, to which the waiver applies, and the waiver shall apply only to the work and uses so identified. In the case of a joint work prepared by two or more authors, a waiver of rights under this paragraph made by one such author waives such rights for all such authors.

(2) Ownership of the rights conferred by subsection (a) with respect to a work of visual art is distinct from ownership of any copy of that work, or of a copyright or any exclusive right under a copyright in that work. Transfer of ownership of any copy or a work of visual art, or of a copyright or any exclusive right under a copyright, shall not constitute a waiver of the rights conferred by subsection (a). Except as may otherwise be agreed by the author in a written instrument signed by the author, a waiver of the rights conferred by subsection (a) with respect to a work of visual art shall not constitute a transfer of ownership of any copy of that work, or of ownership of a copyright or of any exclusive right under a copyright in that work.

§ 107. Limitations on exclusive rights: Fair use

Notwithstanding the provisions of sections 106 and 106A, the fair use of a copyrighted work, including such use by reproduction in copies or phonorecords or by any other means specified by that section, for purposes such as criticism, comment, news reporting, teaching (including multiple copies for classroom use), scholarship, or research, is not an infringement of copyright. In determining whether the use made of a work in any particular case is a fair use the factors to be considered shall include -

- (1) the purpose and character of the use, including whether such use is of a commercial nature or is for nonprofit educational purposes;
- (2) the nature of the copyrighted work;
- (3) the amount and substantiality of the portion used in relation to the copyrighted work as a whole; and
- (4) the effect of the use upon the potential market for or value of the copyrighted work. The fact that a work is unpublished shall not itself bar a finding of fair use if such finding is made upon consideration of all the above factors.

About the Author

Cheryl Besenjak began her career in copyright in the Copyright and Permissions Department at Scott, Foresman and Company in 1983, now known as ScottForesman. In 1990 she founded The Permissions Group, a full-service rights and permissions consulting company. She is publisher of *copyRights©*—the national newsletter on rights and permissions. Cheryl is an active member of Chicago Women in Publishing.

Cheryl has woven her active professional life in and around her family and church. She lives with her husband, Joe, daughter Kate, and their black lab Rebecca in a suburb of Chicago where she especially enjoys singing in the choir of Holy Trinity Lutheran Church. Her grown sons Roger and Brian live in downstate Illinois.

Index